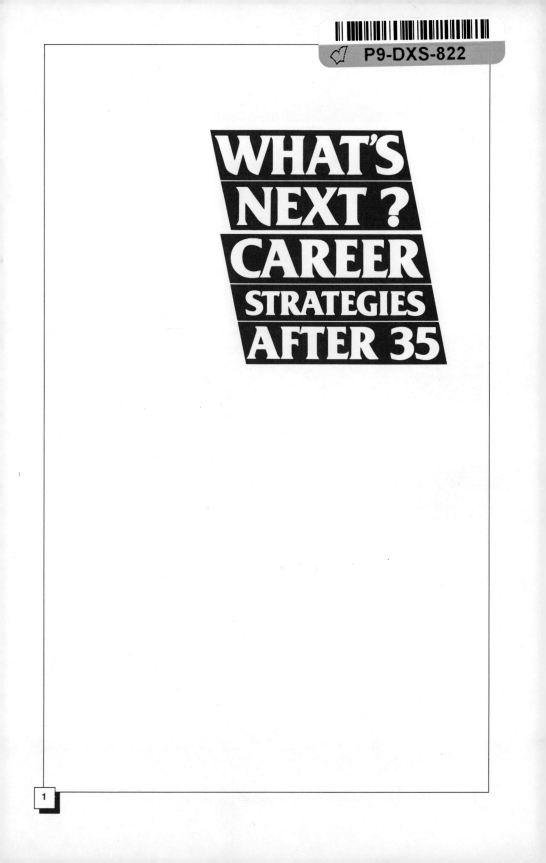

WHAT'S NEXT? CAREER STRATEGIES AFTER 35

WHAT'S NEXT ?
CAREER STRATEGIES AFTER 35

JACK FALVEY

WILLIAMSON PUBLISHING
CHARLOTTE, VERMONT 05445

Library of Congress Cataloging-in-Publication Data

Falvey, Jack, 1938–
  What's Next?

  Bibliography: p.
  Includes index.
1. Career changes. I. Title.
HF5384.F35   1987   650.1'4   87-10553
ISBN 0-913589-26-8
Cover and interior design: Trezzo-Braren Studio
Typography: Villanti & Sons, Printers, Inc.
Printing: Capital City Press

Williamson Publishing Co.
Charlotte, Vermont 05445

Manufactured in the United States of America

To Mary, Kris, Jim and Ellen
who have shared my
career strategies both
before and after 35.

ACKNOWLEDGEMENTS

Although perceived as a solitary pursuit, writing a book is a group endeavor. Jack Williamson and Susan Williamson as publisher and editor are the major players on the team. A year's worth of give and take moved the project along to the product you have in your hands.

Although I find it personally preferable to write in longhand with a pen on a lined pad, a word processor at some point must enter into the picture. The Office, a professional secretarial service, made the electronic transfer through the nimble fingers and diligent minds of Judy Foley, Chris Nagy, Marguerite Martin and Judi Erekson.

Those reading the manuscript or making suggestions for content include Leslie Agnello, Lelija Bird, Anne DeFrancesco, Brenda Duffy, Chris Filip, Betty Lehan Harragan, John Haussler, Bob Hennessey, Pam Heumann, Janet Jordan, Tom O'Loughlin, Steve Rapson, John Strasburger, George Sullivan, and Joe Taylor.

Special thanks go to V.J. Pappas and Tony Lee of *National Business Employment Weekly*, as well as former staff Russ Bleemer and Ellen Kolton. Each of these professionals has contributed to my writing in the career field.

Finally, this book could not have been written without the many people who have shared their career dilemmas and stories over the past twelve years.

CONTENTS

If one advances confidently in the direction of his dreams, and endeavors to live the life which he has imagined, he will meet with a success unexpected in common hours. THOREAU

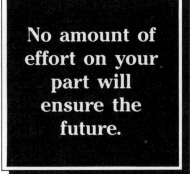

No amount of effort on your part will ensure the future.

Are you somewhere in the corporate zoo? Are you beginning to notice that the fat cats in the corner cages of the lion house are fed much larger quantities of red meat than you seem to be getting in the monkey house? Have you observed that very few monkeys ever go to the lion house (and some of those that do go are eaten alive)? Congratulations, you are beginning to focus on reality! Be grateful for the perception. The more vivid your view, the more courage it will generate. This type of courage leads to taking action on your own behalf. This book is about the kinds of action you should take.

Okay, you're somewhere in the Fortune five million; you slug it out on a day-to-day basis, just trying to get your job done and earn a living. But you have a feeling there may be something more to life. There is! Now is the time to find out what it might be.

> **Begin to manage your career rather than have it, and pure chance, manage you.**

Sometime after your first decade of career experiences, it's wise to take a look at what you have done, where you have been, how things have developed or failed to develop. Take these observations and focus them forward.

A few false starts, a couple of funny twists and turns find their way into everyone's life. Things don't work out either exactly as planned, nor do they follow some textbook model. No amount of effort on your part will ensure the future. No one manages to create a plan for life and then uneventfully proceed to live it "to the letter." What you can do is recognize the options, as slight as they may be at times, and begin to manage your career rather than have it, and pure chance, manage you. You can cut your losses. You can discover the occasional golden opportunity. You can make a few adjustments. You can be in control to a greater degree than you might think. You can take what you have experienced and learned, and work it against what the future has to offer.

Wherever you are, or whoever you are right now, if you have the feeling that there could be more to your career than forty more years of "business as usual," you are ready to open yourself up to what might be.

AS YOU LIKE IT

There is nothing wrong with hard work and slow steady progress in life. The world requires vast numbers of people to keep it going each day. Many people are already operating at the top of their game doing precisely the things they are now doing. Generally, they are more than happy with their mission in life and are performing a vital part of the overall balance. On the other hand, if you have the feeling that you have more to offer, could move a little faster, could be more productive for yourself and your work, then it's time to begin to think about increasing both your contributions and your payoffs.

By the time you reach your mid-thirties, you may not have all the answers but most of the questions have now become more clearly defined. You know your strengths. You also know the areas you'd do best to avoid. While some people seem to have it made, in reality they often don't. You understand that even in reaching the so-called "top", the end result often isn't worth the price paid in time and effort.

> **By the time you reach your mid-thirties, you may not have all the answers but most of the questions have now become more clearly defined.**

> **Reality quickly removes the aura of glamour.**

If you are close to the people who a few years ago were your career role models in high places with great power, you now can probably see that they are not super men and women, but just players like you, just a few steps or years ahead in the game. They have personal lives, they make mistakes, they have made career commitments, they have made moves. Where they are now may not be where you want to be (or even where they wish to be) considering what it takes to get and to stay there. Flying the red-eye in from the coast for a big meeting may seem like the epitome of action and excitement. That is only true before you have actually had the chance to do it a couple of times. Reality quickly removes the aura of glamour.

By now you probably have seen, heard, and sensed enough to understand the price of the career goals that looked so distant and awesome only a few years before. You now know many of the unwritten rules of the game.

You may not be able to win that game. You may wisely reason that it's not worth the price. But you do have the chance to work on your own definition of winning rather than following someone else's norm.

The time is now right (perhaps for the first time) for taking a serious shot at answering the question: What are you going to be when you grow up?

CHAPTER 1

A MOSAIC, NOT A BLUEPRINT

> **Instead of trying to create the ideal resume, why not consider trying to create the ideal biography?**

Instead of trying to create the ideal resume, why not consider trying to create the ideal biography? One is for someone else's subjective evaluation, the other is for your own benefit and enjoyment.

The plural in the title of this book, "strategies," indicates that you are dealing with multiple paths, many decisions, all kinds of ideas, large numbers of alternatives and the acceptance that life, and the passage through it, has little science or certainty. In return for life's lack of predictability, there are all kinds of surprises (many of them good ones), unknowns (some of them fun to learn about), and some twists and turns that have made biographies exciting reading for centuries. How will your biography read? You may be able to fill it with more action than you think.

INSIGHTFUL PATTERNS

Having multiple answers to the question of what you are going to be when you grow up will allow you to pick the best direction at any given time, even at mid-life or later, and shift easily to other opportunities which may come your way. An open view of where you might be going allows for greater growth, a wider spectrum of change, and more spontaneity.

This approach alters many of the accepted rules of career progress. You do not work from blueprints with all the engineered parts fitting together in some preplanned design.

What really happens is you accumulate all kinds of odd pieces from your life's experience and careers. You meet an assortment of people, you are exposed to great numbers of situations and many, many challenges.

Your responses, your reactions, and your efforts as well as your blood, sweat, and tears build a unique background. Fitting all these pieces into some kind of mosaic pattern gives added meaning to your past, and sheds an energizing light on the future. Many pieces will seem to be left over or left out; others will surprise you in their uncharacteristic, yet newly appropriate fit. Few will be wasted because they somehow pull you into areas of useful application. You needn't try too hard to see an overall picture or pattern in your personal mosaic, as it is ever-evolving. What you want to gain is a sense of accomplishment and a feeling of potential from what you have done.

Does the concept of flexibility have validity? Must every move you make have solid preplanned career implications? What is the value of freedom of choice if you don't exercise it? At any stage of life it is okay to explore, to look beyond the day-to-day, to see what may be out there. Little or no career damage will be done. Life patterns can often be rejoined or reestablished. You may not have the unencumbered freedom to make broad spontaneous moves, but fear of breaking what you perceive as a standard career path should not hold you rigidly in place.

Fear of breaking what you perceive as a standard career path should not hold you rigidly in place.

Fitting all these pieces into some kind of mosaic pattern gives added meaning to our pasts, and sheds an energizing light on the future.

Somewhere between being a frivolous career nomad or being an industrial drone is a vast mid-ground of colorful experiences that make up the pieces used to construct a personal free-form career mosaic. Understanding the nature of the assembly process will allow you to look more closely at ideas or opportunities that present themselves. Seeing what's out there should cause you to work more diligently at getting free of the situations that box you in and limit your freedom and choices. The degree of freedom we each achieve will vary greatly from time to time in our careers, but creating space to maneuver, no matter how tight things seem to be, is always worth the effort and temporary discomfort.

> **Fear of failure is a far more powerful force and, in many cases, a more damaging one than failure itself.**

FEAR OF FAILURE— THE NUMBER ONE ENEMY!

One of the major forces that keep people from taking any action on their own behalf is fear. Fear of failure is a far more powerful force and, in many cases, a more damaging one than failure itself.

Failure, while very real, is vastly overrated in the damage it can do. It's rarely permanent. One man formed a partnership in his field and had it working fairly well when, through unforeseen circumstances, the business took a downturn and failed. In the process, he lost his investment which included his house. He had to feed his family, so he found a job, a place to rent, and pressed on. He was not bitter, just sadder and wiser. It took him almost ten years to become a homeowner once again but those were not miserable years of grinding it out. He went to work, did his job, found an occasional outside project to gain a little extra income, and kept his eyes open for a chance to do it all again if possible.

He is a highly skilled professional manager who has a realistic view of his strengths and what it takes to make it in an independent business. As his family grows and his resources build, he may give it another shot. He is doing well in his current position by almost anyone's standards. Even when things do not work in storybook fashion, they still work out. Our perception and projection of how we might handle a failed situation is as unrealistic as our perception of what success and its perks will bring. The sun still rises every twenty-four hours in both situations.

The challenge is to *make* things work out rather than to *hope* they will work out. Assuming responsibility no matter what the result is better than not taking the initiative. You will have difficulty transforming yourself into something you are not. That is not what must be done. What you want to become is an observer of what's going on, of how things work, of how you can make them work for you, and last but not least, of what you bring to the equation and what you can do with what you have to offer. Determining your strengths and how best to make a contribution is an unending challenge. The answers will continue to change. Just keep asking the questions.

You don't have to go out on your own, start your own business, or leave the corporate world to be in

> **Even when things do not work in storybook fashion, they still work out.**

> **Assuming responsibility no matter what the result is better than not taking the initiative.**

> **Few results of value can be achieved without some risk and some price being paid.**

> **You now know that you are not just someone with potential. You are someone with substance.**

> **The world has always worked to put down those who see themselves with talent or potential. Don't accept that message.**

> **Think for a while about what might be.**

charge of who you are and what you do. You may have to move around a bit, but few results of value can be achieved without some risk and some price being paid.

You have been around long enough to understand how things work. You have learned through observation and occasionally by some hard lessons.

You now know that you are not just someone with potential. You are someone with substance. How much substance may vary, but your own opinion of how much substance and ability you have should begin to mean more to you than someone else's opinion.

Knowing what is going on and doing something about it is what is required. Knowing your limitations and the strength of the adversary are important, but you must be careful not to overestimate the power of these two elements or they will induce paralysis. In general, you can count on being of more value and stronger than you give yourself credit for. The world has always worked to put down those who see themselves with talent or potential. Don't accept that message. Try getting your mind outside of the day-to-day reality for a few minutes; it's a healthy exercise that has led more than one person off in some new direction. Think for a while about what might be.

YOUR CAREER WISH LIST

In the world of fables and folklore, the plots of stories with genies usually revolve around someone being granted three wishes.

The fantasy of instant gratification doesn't come true too often in the real world, but that is not the objective if you think about it. Still, the fable can be much closer to reality than you think. It may be a little frightening to consider, but the fact is if you make wishes (set some objectives), the chances of them coming true are increased. Not wishes like finding a buried treasure or winning the lottery, but wishes about something over which you have influence. The psychology of self-fulfilling prophecies has been known for some time. Men and women have been goal-directed throughout recorded time. The one thing that slows up progress more than any other is the failure to set any kind of goal or objective.

When discussing careers, people often say something like "I don't know what I want to do." That is understandable because the options open are almost limitless, or, in some cases, the boxes we have built ourselves into seem almost airtight. The problems come when you fail to begin exploring what you might like to do. Finding goals isn't as narrow as the choice of only three wishes; after all, when it comes to careers, you have as many wishes as you want. You also have the freedom to change your objectives along the way as you learn more about yourself and the environment in which you work.

You can make no choices at all if you would like. That means, in effect, that you are choosing your present circumstances. But if you feel that there should be something more to life, then the question is what?

> **The one thing that slows up progress more than any other is the failure to set any kind of goal or objective.**

> **Past experience isn't a solid indicator of future performance.**

Experience can be gained just about overnight, though there are those who would like you to believe differently.

EXPERIENCE IS NOT ALWAYS THE BEST INDICATOR

Don't get your objectives hung up on what you have been able to do in the past. Past experience isn't a solid indicator of future performance. Experience can be gained rapidly once an opportunity is secured. Thousands of people have made major moves completely unsupported by previous experience. Don't block your thought processes with an invalid assumption. You don't have to think about making a radical move, but at least open your eyes a bit wider.

Personnel types like to hire people according to experience profiles when, in fact, most people are capable of fitting into almost any situation. Social skills, an open mind, and enthusiasm are always welcome and much needed. Experience can be gained just about overnight, though there are those who would like you to believe differently.

Generating opportunities in areas where you have no expertise isn't easy to do, but it can be done. Chances are that you probably did it when you entered the working world. Companies recognize that new hires are inexperienced, cheap, and don't know any better. Now that you are older and wiser you can see the fallacy in the statement "I have no experience, so no one wants me." There are enough real limitations to life without adding marginal extras, especially when you are just building a fresh positive mind set.

One college English major became a parole officer when he graduated. He burned out with an overwhelming caseload. Within five years he was a sales vice president at a high tech communications company. In between he sold books; then through two moves and the discovery of a fast-growing company, he was able to arrive at a destination he didn't even dream about a few short months before. Don't limit your wishes by boxing yourself in by what you have done in the past. It's time to "blue-sky" it in this kind of an eye-opening exercise.

> **Don't limit your wishes by boxing yourself in by what you have done in the past.**

> **The biggest battle with any career wish list will be fought between your own two ears.**

GO FOR WHAT YOU WANT

There is little value in aptitude or interest tests (in case you were thinking about them as a first step), because they can only cover a small range of talents and possibilities. They always seem to recommend you become a beekeeper. What you want is what you can get. Finding out what the outside world has to offer is the controlling factor, rather than trying to explore superficially what is inside of you. What is actually inside you will amaze you; it cannot be detected with a pencil and paper. It will eventually require that you put yourself to the real test of giving things a try. The whole business of seeking direction is much more like a treasure hunt than any kind of scientific search. You have to follow the clues. You have to become sensitive to how others have evolved.

The biggest battle with any career wish list will be fought between your own two ears. You have to see yourself as someone who can do almost anything you set out to do. We all have mental and physical limitations, but many of us also have underutilized strengths, some of which we don't even know exist.

Start with the three wish technique. You don't need anyone's permission. Give yourself a break and begin to see what is out there. Finding something without looking is possible, but becoming a student of possibilities greatly increases your chances of discovering some real, not just wishful, options.

Look around you. How did those people get there? Someone undoubtedly has a "classic" tale. One of my favorite stories is about a couple I know; the wife was recruited for a high-paying sales job at a computer communications software company. She had decided to drop out of the workforce to complete a difficult pregnancy, and, instead of letting the new job opportunity go to waste, passed the information on to her husband (remember the parole officer turned book salesman?). He took her interview, got the job and today is vice president of the company. She had the baby and has since gone back to work at another major computer company.

A word of caution to close out this chapter. You must be very careful about sharing your wishes, possible plans, or general feelings with those with whom you work. This is very difficult because business associates tend also to be friends, but it is a vital point. It is human nature to look at the ideas of others and compare them to our own situation. Many people do not want to think too hard about who they are and where they are going. If they have made a personal commitment to their current situation, either willingly or not, they would just as soon not learn about someone with the ability to take charge of his or her own life and perhaps have the chance to move on to bigger and better things. No matter how much you trust your associates the amount of candid feedback and advice you will receive will seldom balance the seed of discontent you may sow. There is, too, the possibility that some of your early thoughts might be inadvertently passed along and thus somehow come back to you in a way that may actually interfere with a future orderly transition.

You have to test the waters and talk about what you are doing or may plan to do. You need outside professional friends for this purpose. Senior level people in other organizations are ideal. We will talk at length about contact networks further on, but if you are about to close this book and head into work tomorrow morning, your innermost thoughts on some of these ideas may *not* be the best topics of light conversation over coffee.

CHAPTER 2

IT ISN'T EASY

> **Being economically bound to an organization should ring the alarm bells in your mind.**

eople work for love and for money and seldom get enough of either. On occasion you do receive a little more money than expected and that just about locks you in to wherever you are.

The golden handcuffs of the senior management team with their stock options and deferred income plans have a junior, silver handcuffs counterpart that holds many people in place almost against their wills. Being economically bound to an organization should ring the alarm bells in your mind.

The junior handcuff version is easy to understand, if not so easy to break out of. First, although starting salaries may not be the highest, as soon as you begin to show promise, you are designated as a comer or potential high achiever. You aren't given a get-rich-quick program, but you do get substantial increases and bonus opportunities and pay-outs. The place isn't perfect but at least the money is good, right? It is so good, in fact, that you most likely couldn't do as well anywhere else.

> **Human nature allows us to live up to our income with very few adjustment difficulties.**

Human nature allows us to live up to our income with very few adjustment difficulties. Middle management, and sometimes top management, know that by keeping skilled people on the high end of their salary scale, they effectively prevent them from leaving. Cash is the glue that holds the place together. It's not that you couldn't do amost as well elsewhere, it's just that it's pretty near impossible to earn an added ten or fifteen percent more by making a move, because you are already at the top of the market for your level or position. And so there you sit, figuratively, if not physically, locked in.

> **Early retirement is the euphemism for paying people off and getting rid of them.**

LOOK AHEAD

The hours may be unbelievable, the travel excessive, the deadlines unrealistic, but where could you get this kind of money? The answer is nowhere. If you don't eventually burn up or burn out, you may make it to an upper level of the organizational pyramid. Is this really the place you want to be?

The next wave of junior hopefuls is now in the system, somewhat overpayed as you were. Now further along in your career, you are sitting on a substantial income with all the appropriate personal financial obligations (perhaps a family and mortgage). An organization can do much better for itself by cutting high-cost talent if and when business cycles turn down, and they always will. Early retirement is the euphemism for paying people off and getting rid of them. Is this what you are programming yourself for? Your options at fifty or fifty-five are altogether different than at forty or forty-five. These must be considerations as you look at where you are now and where you may be heading.

To be able to see some of this in your thirties is sometimes very difficult. After all, the future may look very bright indeed! One junior manager joined a major multinational in his mid-thirties and a month into the job received an invitation to a retirement party for a third-level manager. The evening was impressive. The chairman of the board paid tribute, a this-is-your-life slide show ran, and friends came in from all across the country to be at the dinner. It wasn't until almost a year later that the new manager realized this had just been a means of cleaning house, of making room for a junior to move up. Its cost was relatively small considering the man's own pension contributions funded much of his reduced income, and the little bridge package that was added on was no more than what a reasonable severance and outplacement program would have cost the company. He was only fifty-eight, although he looked much older and, of course, to the junior manager he looked very old indeed. Being a cast-off before sixty isn't much of a career climax. The victim had few options except graceful inactivity.

Being transferred to a division just before it is sold or dissolved is another housekeeping tactic that takes care of high-priced but used talent. The club gets smaller and harder to belong to even if you have the ability to keep pace. The arrival of a chief executive from the outside, for whatever reason, automatically ends the careers of multiple senior managers in that organization. Performance has nothing to do with fate.

The issue here is who is in control of what? Organizations, by their very nature, build dependence.

> **Performance has nothing to do with fate.**

> **Organizations, by their very nature, build dependence.**

Economic, social, promotional, all-encompassing dependence can be highly hazardous to one's career health. All the eggs in one basket has always carried great risk. Recognizing the pervasiveness of the situation is important. "I will give this job another three years." "In five years I will look for a start-up outfit." "As soon as I can get some capital saved, I would like to start something on my own." All of these extended thoughts assume the acceptance of the current situation. Being uneasy with the status quo, no matter how superficially comfortable, is critical. The present leads to the future, and organizations have highly predictable futures.

MAINTAINING ECONOMIC OPTIONS

Taking a hard look at economics and opportunities early in your career will give you options later on that will be of great value.

If you have a dual-income from a spouse, it can buy maneuver time in making career moves. A double paycheck upsets some of the lock-in factors and allows both partners to be able to make moves that each as individuals couldn't manage, provided the couple isn't living up to its last penny or beyond.

Your perception of your income and lifestyle is usually somewhat inflated. You only have to be out of work for six or nine months to realize that you can get along on considerably less income during trying times.

It's not necessary to have a year or two base salary in the bank. That's beyond reach for even the most controlled individual.

You should think in terms of keeping overhead down so that if you had to take your existing twelve-month income figure and stretch it out over fifteen to eighteen months, you might be able to do it.

Again, it's not recommended that you leave one income source until you have another lined up, but creating some economic breathing space will allow you to manage an unexpected transition more reasonably. It could even give you the option of going after another opportunity full time for a few months if the situation dictated.

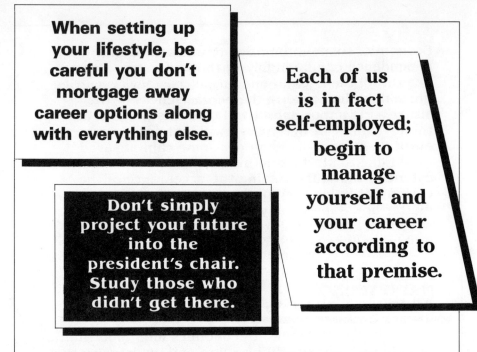

When setting up your lifestyle, be careful you don't mortgage away career options along with everything else.

Each of us is in fact self-employed; begin to manage yourself and your career according to that premise.

Don't simply project your future into the president's chair. Study those who didn't get there.

Getting financially established is costly. When setting up your lifestyle, be careful you don't mortgage away career options along with everything else. If you already feel you have, then take a closer look; very likely there are some "necessities" that you can live without.

The good news is that you can do much more than you think you can, with far less than you think, for much longer than you think, if you will just take some time to look over where your career might be leading you. Don't simply project your future into the president's chair. Study those who didn't get there. They, by their numbers alone, will be easier to approach and analyze. Avoid or minimize a mid-life career crisis by taking more control over who you are and where you are going while the choices are more numerous and the consequences are easier to deal with.

Each of us is in fact self-employed; begin to manage yourself and your career according to that premise. Marketing your services to a single customer is never a sound business practice. Even if you can only sell yourself to one organization at a time, having a list of future customers (employers) and keeping lines open in those directions is a minimal safety system.

Doing your economic homework and managing your lifestyle will open up options that will allow you to keep the keys to your own handcuffs, either silver or gold. Becoming completely independent may be unrealistic, but reducing your degree of dependency a few steps at a time should be part of your overall career strategy.

BROADENING YOUR VIEW

If economics are a real but manageable restraint on what you can do, background can also seem to be a lock-out factor in career strategies. Fortunately, this apparent obstacle can also be overcome. You have to look a step or two beyond the obvious in some cases, but that is always a requirement of sound self-management.

Industry experience is vastly overrated. General business, social, professional, and organizational skills transfer easily across all kinds of professions and ventures. When an industry for some reason winds down, it's instructive to see in how many different directions its former inhabitants end up going.

Twenty-five years in one company or industry is often viewed negatively. People who build resumes construct linear progression charts that appear to lead step by endless step right to the top. You already know it rarely works this way. If longevity were the answer and going through the steps were how it is done, there would never be any new ideas, new companies, new opportunities, or most likely, human progress. Don't be afraid of broadening your view.

> **When an industry for some reason winds down, it's instructive to see in how many different directions its former inhabitants end up going.**

Don't be afraid of broadening your view.

At least you know that it can be done. In some highly insular industries and companies, it may be just about impossible to break through background requirements, but that will be their loss, not yours. Reality is on your side. Probing for a new line of least resistance is better than spending ten or twenty years stringing together some idealized set of moves which have no inherent career guarantees.

If you want proof of the concept of cross-industry transferability of skills, just think about the consulting business. Consultants accept clients from the four winds and seldom have difficulty fitting into the flow of the business in a very short time.

The differences in the mechanics of how organizations work from industry to industry are very slight. Everyone will tell you how distinct they are but it just isn't true. The actual barriers to mobility from industry to industry are purely subjective. That doesn't make them easy to overcome. If you have an

The actual barriers to mobility from industry to industry are purely subjective.

It's harder than you might think to get in over your head. Things just are not that complex.

opportunity for a major change, you should not be intimidated by your lack of background. One or two people per company need to be extremely knowledgeable about the technology or intricacies of operations. Everyone else need only have general skills for the area in which they contribute. You may feel locked in to what you are doing and see no way out short of beginning at the bottom of some other profession. The picture is somewhat brighter than that. It's harder than you might think to get in over your head. Things just are not that complex. Again building the bridge, getting the opportunity, actually making a move are what's difficult. Once you have arrived, the learning curve will be steep but, in almost all cases, manageable.

All of the obstacles to mobility and career strategies can be overcome, but not without considerable effort. Breaking out of a difficult situation, or even a comfortable situation, is seldom easy. Doing all of the things necessary to explore options, developing a workable financial base for a move, making contacts to go around subjective credential or experience requirements—all can be done. Because they seem to be such formidable challenges, few people are willing to put out the energy needed to manage their way through a planned transition. Upsetting the status quo takes a lot of inner strength. Interestingly, when the transition is unplanned (someone gets fired, cut back, or for any reason must make an unexpected move), somehow then the reserves necessary to survive are summoned. That means they are there for most people. You just have to recognize the logic of calling up what is needed on your own behalf when an immediate emergency isn't present.

By continuing to do what you are doing, you are covered as far as not missing whatever good may develop where you are. What requires discipline and desire is to put yourself in the running for opportunities that can be explored outside of your current working environment. Others have overcome the economic and comfort level obstacles. They have been able to make cross-industry moves. Are there any reasons why you can't take a look in those directions as well?

You can sense the barriers. Some are real—formidable but surmountable. Others are more of your own making in your mind's eye. These may be more difficult to overcome but certainly it's possible. Try not to concentrate on immediate barriers. Begin by raising the level of your thinking beyond the difficult foreground. Envision what may be out there that will make an effort worthwhile. Before you develop all the "why nots" take a longer look at the possibilities. Turning them into probabilities can be done.

> **Before you develop all the "why nots" take a longer look at the possibilities.**

CHAPTER 3

SECURITY IS WITHIN

> **A job for life, a no layoff policy, tenure, or early retirement are not career goals. They are life sentences.**

Locking in your planned future is also locking out your potential future. A job for life, a no layoff policy, tenure, or early retirement are not career goals. They are life sentences.

Once you change your view of security from something provided by organizations to something created by yourself from within yourself, then you will begin to be able to address career issues in ways that will provide lasting versus temporary answers.

Playing in the organizational lottery, trying to pick a mover to become associated with, are approaches that produce far more losers than winners. Attaching yourself to a star in the hope of being pulled along with him or her is risky at best. You have little or no control over whether that person will actually be a shooting star or a falling star.

Real job security is having the ability, confidence, vision, courage, and skill necessary to get an economic return on what you bring to the marketplace.

It's instructive to study the moves of immigrants who came to the United States over the last hundred years with little more than the clothes on their backs. Unable to speak the language, often having to suffer racial and religious prejudice, they took the low-level labor jobs available to them in order to gain the footing to start small businesses so that their sons and daughters could become educated and join the establishment that they themselves were not allowed to enter.

Think about the paradox. These people provided their own security. They understood the things that had to be done and did them. They understood the concept of self-generated security even if they couldn't define it.

You don't have to be very far along in management to know that business is an inexact science at best and an almost black art with no rhyme or reason at worst. Business—whole industries—come and go with little regard to the contributions of those working in them, let alone any means of providing for their futures.

Your future belongs to you. That isn't bad news; that's good news. Your challenge is not unlike that of the immigrants. What has to be done and how do you get paid for doing it?

The economic ladder can be climbed to whatever level your ability and ambition will carry you. The price you must pay is almost always tied in some way to the level you aim for. An odd characteristic of our system seems to be that the efforts required at the very bottom and the very top are almost equal, one for survival, the other for prominence as well as survival of a different sort.

BE WHERE THE ACTION IS

The basics of business require that a product or service be developed and delivered to a customer in return for payment. The closer you are to the fundamentals of that process, the more valuable your contribution. The further away in support or peripheral activities, the less valuable and more expendable you become. In different industries, different disciplines are of differing degrees of importance. Part of the challenge of self-reliance is to determine where the action is. What's important? What produces the revenue? Who runs the show? You must match your strengths to the basics of a business. You are the single most adaptable organism on the face of the earth. Gravitate in the direction of those functions that produce results. Staff support, while emotionally rewarding, is one of the most dangerous positions in the career spectrum. If you are in it, get out. If you

> **The closer you can position yourself to the fundamentals of a given endeavor, the more value you will contribute.**

have to leave your current position to do so, do it. Far better that you leave it, than the other way around.

The closer you can position yourself to the fundamentals of a given endeavor the more value you will contribute. If you have the mentality and drive to found a business, you, of course, become its driving force, and if you are careful in how you set things up, its chief benefactor. If you are the number two person or part of the start-up team and can make the various transitions that growth requires, then you benefit accordingly (with a piece of the action). If your technical know-how is a big element and you can keep up with or ahead of the state-of-the-art, you are also golden. These are all fundamental slots.

If you bring in the sales in a meaningful way—and that is a critical element—in most cases, there again, you have or can bring basic value to the party. It's when you start getting off the main line and begin to get into public relations, or data processing, or (God help you) personnel, that you begin to become expendable. If you further specialize in some small segment of a field, the market for your services becomes that much more narrow. Your future will always depend on the impact your contribution will bring to a situation. Think in terms of fundamental impact versus support positions.

> **Your future will always depend on the impact your contribution will bring to a situation.**

ANALYZE FOR
CRITICAL ELEMENTS

Big companies tend to segment jobs into small specialities, and it is easy to lose sight of reality once you are entangled in some minute cell of the organism.

Learning to identify the critical elements in any business in order that you might be able to either provide one, or be close to one, is a skill you must cultivate. It's difficult to be *where* the action is if you don't even know *what* the action is.

Think about critical business elements. Fast food has little to do with food. It is a real estate, marketing and franchising business in its current state of development. High technology, while still black box-software driven, is making a transition into a base industry with all its generalist and peripheral positions.

> **Think about critical business elements. Fast food has little to do with food.**

R&D, sales, and finance are still the key elements. Airlines and hotels are capital-intensive, people-service industries that incidentally operate seven days a week, twenty-four hours a day. Managing people, managing money, managing systems, and managing the people that manage all of the above are areas that are fundamental across most industries.

Constantly analyzing these elements in each field you encounter, and matching yourself up against the requirements, will begin to lead you towards the strengths you can build on and work at as part of your internal career security system. What you can do, how important it is, how much fundamental impact it has on corporate success is what contributes to long-term security.

You must think of yourself as a free-standing economic entity. What are the things that you do that can make a contribution? In mid-career you have already made substantial contributions in order to earn a living. Being aware of what you do well and how it has fit with an overall operation is a good first step in beginning to think about yourself in terms of an independent versus dependent person. None of us is completely independent of the economic system. Even those who are independently wealthy must constantly monitor and manage wealth and that becomes a job in itself. Think of yourself as an independent contractor selling your services to your current employer. You must understand what you do and its relation to the whole to know if your service can have greater value elsewhere. You must be confident enough in what you do to be able to sell those services elsewhere, if circumstances dictate. That is a giant step in perception from the idea of finding a "secure" job in a "well-established" company and delegating your progress through life to that organization.

> **You must think of yourself as a free-standing economic entity.**

> **You must understand what you do and its relation to the whole to know if your service can have greater value elsewhere.**

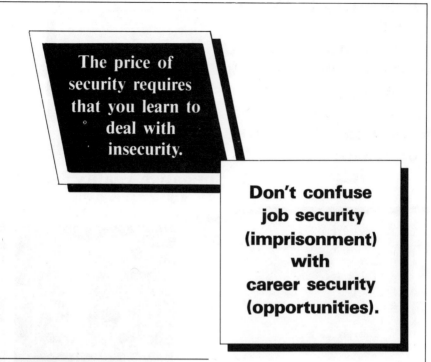

The price of
security requires
that you learn to
deal with
insecurity.

Don't confuse
job security
(imprisonment)
with
career security
(opportunities).

JOB SECURITY
COMES FROM WITHIN

The price of security requires that you learn to deal with insecurity.

One big company manager used to take out his wallet on occasion and look at his union card, earned many years before as a riveter in an aircraft factory. He was fond of saying that if things didn't work out he had a trade. As it turned out he was fired in his early forties in a management cutback. He then realized that he had a management trade as well as the comforting riveter trade, and he found another organization in which to make a managerial contribution. Knowing what your contribution really is and how it can be transferred across industries will begin to shed light on your potential career security. Don't confuse job security (imprisonment) with career security (opportunities).

Little reflections of insecurity are used defensively by many people against the specter of unemployment. What they fear may be a downward slide on the economic scale.

> **Insecurity is the paralyzing factor, which not only feeds on itself, but holds people in situations far longer than health or reason would dictate.**

> **It's far better to make your own moves in your own time than to have to react to a negative reality.**

> **Setting goals distant enough so that no present action is required is not planning. It is self-delusion.**

Insecurity is the paralyzing factor, which not only feeds on itself, but holds people in situations far longer than health or reason would dictate.

The things you can do to manage your career are fairly straightforward. The questions you must address go beyond the exploration and planning, the contacting and research. You must ask yourself if you are willing to take the risks that flexibility and mobility will require. In truth, you might as well since those who choose not to, often, because of unforeseen organizational changes, must learn to fend for themselves anyway. It's far better to make your own moves in your own time than to have to react to a negative reality.

Time and time again you hear people say that they are planning to start their own business in a few years when they get a few dollars ahead and have enough capital to support themselves for a year or two. That statement in most cases is a forlorn dream created to sustain some hope in what is usually a less than tolerable current situation.

Setting goals distant enough so that no present action is required is not planning. It is self-delusion.

Everyone's career mosaic does not complete itself in self-employment, complete independence, or total security. A career can go through many nonlinear stages. Few things are forever. The patterns are jumbled. The chance meeting of ability, opportunity, and courage can happen at any time, and it can happen many times. The rarest of the three elements is courage. It takes a strong person to take charge of what he or she is doing and where he or she is going. If that person is a single parent, responsible for a family, up to here in debt, and burdened with many of the standard things that life deals out, then the courage factor must multiply itself.

Somewhere between being driven off the deep-end and bouncing around like a rubber ball should be a set of moves that will be at least tolerable, if not comfortable, and will make you a key element in your own security. Self-reliance, not complete independence, is what produces security.

Go back in your career and look at how far you have come. Think about your early experiences. Think about what you have been able to contribute. Make a collection of all of the things you have been able to do successfully. Those are the building blocks for your next moves. Those are the mosaic pieces you have to work with. Those are the elements that will provide security and reinforcement.

> **Self-reliance, not complete independence, is what produces security.**

> **The chance meeting of ability, opportunity, and courage can happen at any time, and it can happen many times.**

Even though everything you may have done has been done for a company or within an organization, it has still been done by you. It was your contribution. You know how to contribute.

Where and how to sell that ability to contribute without selling yourself short is what career security is all about.

Knowing that you can contribute in a meaningful way will allow you to break free of the organizational security myth.

> **Even though everything you may have done has been done for a company or within an organization, it has still been done by you. It was your contribution. You know how to contribute.**

CHAPTER 4

SMALL, MEDIUM, OR LARGE?

> **One factor that seems constant is that big organizations move slowly. They also take a long time to die.**

You may already have a preference or even think you know precisely what size company you prefer, but as you develop your strategies, keep in mind the basic differences that size dictates in the nature of organizations.

There is no ideal. Small outfits are always struggling to get to medium-size so that they can survive. Medium-sized companies are always trying to get organized so that they can become large. Large companies are always struggling to regain the spirit and flexibility they had when they were small and medium. And so it goes.

They are always in motion. Exactly where a company is in its growth curve is difficult to detect, as anyone investing in the stock market can tell you. When you join an organization you are doing much more than just buying its stock; you are investing your total professional being, so it is best to go in with your eyes as wide open as possible.

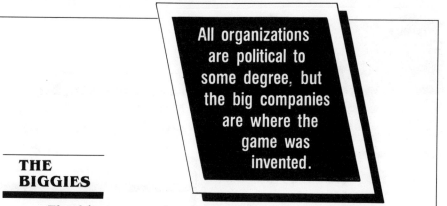

All organizations
are political to
some degree, but
the big companies
are where the
game was
invented.

THE BIGGIES

The big companies generate the most ink in the business press, so they would seem to be the easiest to study. Unfortunately, the business press is subject to all kinds of bias from investor relations, the ego of the C.E.O., industry perceptions, and a myriad of factors that cloud the public's picture.

One division of a big outfit may be dominant. If you are not in soap with Proctor and Gamble or Chevrolet with General Motors, you may just as well not be there at all. Your discipline can be critical. Polaroid draws its top talent from R&D and manufacturing. IBM brings people along through sales. All of these factors shift from time to time just to add to the risk.

One factor that seems constant is that big organizations move slowly. They also take a long time to die. Whatever happens, high-speed decisions on your part are not a requirement. Forty-eight-month calendars are only found in giant organizations.

Big companies are bureaucratic by nature. To survive you must build skills to deal with detailed and unnecessarily complex procedures.

All organizations are political to some degree, but the big companies are where the game was invented. Before each decision or action is taken, the big company person must ask the question, "What are the political consequences of this action?" This step is terribly time-consuming, but it is a fact of life that is ignored at great professional peril.

Real power in big organizations is held at much higher levels than is either wise or necessary. Resources are awesome, but access to those resources can only be had by degree and with multiple approvals.

The investment of time and effort to gain real power and control in big companies is by any measure

> **Being *from* a big company is far better than being *with* a big company.**

> **Budgets are big, benefits can be all encompassing, but there is no free lunch.**

> **The greatest career value of a big company is its name recognition, when after the fact you say you once were with them.**

excessive. Even those who succeed usually spend their entire working life in pursuit of that power and then only hold it for a few years at the end of their long careers.

Being *from* a big company is far better than being *with* a big company.

Big companies have "promote from within only" policies. They create single-track minds which must learn to deal with single-faceted people. It's not a very stimulating long-term environment.

Hiring criteria are often highly cosmetic and social, so you do tend to meet and work with some very "nice" people. There are few renegades. There is little local color. Standards are high but somewhat bland. Boredom sets in sooner rather than later.

The greatest career value of a big company is its name recognition, when after the fact you say you once were with them.

The comfort level of being a junior or middle manager in a big company is almost anesthetic in nature. It dulls the senses and makes one unaware of life outside of the corporate womb. A couple of transcontinental rides on the corporate jet can produce almost complete corporate hypnosis.

Budgets are big, benefits can be all encompassing, but there is no free lunch.

Big company careers carry extremely long odds on winning, only slightly shorter odds on placing, and reasonable odds on a very far-distant show position. The decision point as to how you are doing in the race comes either mercifully very early or cruelly very late in the game. For some people (let's hope you're not one of them), this is still the best game in town. Keep in mind that the vast majority of mid-career decisions are made in favor of leaving the big company. The pyramid nature of organizations in general and the relative small number of major corporations in particular may have a lot to do with this fact, but the exodus of talent cannot be denied.

Retiring as a regional manager or a division vice president after thirty-five years perhaps isn't all that bad, but what was the day-to-day of that thirty-five years really like? If you work out the numbers of just how many people were hired over those many years who did not make it even to those modest levels, it becomes evident that the vast majority of long-term big company players can't and don't win.

IS MEDIUM-SIZE JUST RIGHT?

If you have the skill and ability to make it in a big company, imagine what you could do in a medium-size outfit!

The best of all worlds lies in a company large enough to have some promise of stability even with normal ups and downs, but not so big as to completely stifle individuality and creativity. When you go medium, you give up name recognition and market dominance for a chance to have more impact on what is going on.

Keep in mind that the vast majority of mid-career decisions are made in favor of leaving the big company.

When you go medium, you give up name recognition and market dominance for a chance to have more impact on what is going on.

Medium-size companies tend to more often be family-owned, so unless you plan on becoming a member of the family directly (and not just figuratively), you have to beware of that substantial drawback.

The vast numbers of medium-sized organizations create opportunities in every geographic area. They are headquartered everywhere, not just in four or five major cities. If location is a factor, medium is the answer. Business moves get tiring after a while. You don't learn much or develop greatly by going from one end of the country to the other. Along about mid-career, it's not a bad idea to begin considering locational stability as a factor of increasing strategic importance.

> **If location is a factor, medium is the answer.**

> **The individualists and mavericks that could not find a comfortable home with big companies are found all through medium companies.**

Mid-size outfits move a little faster and therefore require a different sense of how to manage. There are no big staff studies to back up each decision. Reliance on the talents of individuals rather than systems is characteristic. The individualists and mavericks that could not find a comfortable home with big companies are found all through medium companies. You must learn to manage less-than-perfect people—less-than-perfect, that is, in the Fortune 500 sense. These people often produce results far in excess of their apparent talent or their profile-perfect big company counterparts. That has, one would suspect, something to do with that intangible "creative environment," and a sense of personal responsibility which flourishes in mid-size companies. Not being totally "organized" has some hidden benefits.

Medium-sized companies do not run on momentum. They must be operated. There is no automatic pilot. These are hands-on, hand-run enterprises. A highly rewarding complete career can be had in one or more medium-sized companies. Working for more than one company in your career is usually desirable so as not to become inbred, blocked, or pigeon-holed because of early mistakes or stereotyping. When considering medium-sized, take a good look at the product or service, past record of flexibility, the desirable lack of family ownership, the location, and the people you would be working for and with. Then see what kind of a payout you can get for your services.

Again, the numbers alone will tell you that medium-size is not a bad place to be.

> **If the potential is present for ownership, go for it, but go for it up-front.**

> **A piece of the action has been promised to more people joining small businesses than there are grains of sand on the beach.**

IS SMALL TOO RISKY?

Small is always risky so payouts must be quicker and better. A piece of the action has been promised to more people joining small businesses than there are grains of sand on the beach. A promise is never a good deal. Time investments must be brief. It's either going to work in six months or you must be gone.

If the potential is present for ownership, go for it, but go for it up front. Get ground rules in writing. You don't need an iron-clad contract, but you do need a memo of understanding. Changing rules in mid-game is a characteristic of small business. Be careful of entering a partnership where the exit procedure has not been worked out. Whether it's a legal partnership or just a small number of people trying to make a go of an enterprise, it's critical to know, and have spelled out, just what each one's contribution is going to be.

Small businesses are marriages. You live with them. You have to be good at ups and downs because they are a fact of life. Small businesses often require investments. If you are investing your career and putting that at risk, beware of getting in over your head by getting everything you own in there as well. That's the kind of total risk that is best avoided.

There is, of course, the possibility that you will not only do well in a small business, but get the further pleasure of developing it into a medium or even big company. Everything had to start somewhere.

In small business you must work as much with the known and as little with the unknown as possible. You usually are not allowed to make any mistakes; therefore, ultraconservative strategies are the only ones that permit survival long enough to be able to be innovative. Customers are the focus. That's where the money must come from.

THE START-UP BUSINESS

The excitement or emotional drain of small business (depending upon how you look at it) is unmatched except by its subcategory of start-up business. Here the only rule is cash flow. Money must be coming in faster than it is going out. Increasing one, while reducing or controlling the other, is all you have to be concerned with. If you have worked in large and medium-sized companies in the past, you will be amazed how much you can get done with how little resources in how short a period of time in a small start-up company. Small companies require the constant maintenance of career plan B.

> **Small companies require the constant maintenance of career plan B.**

Your own start-up, of course, is the ultimate small business. The rules are maddeningly simple and incredibly difficult.

Your own start-up, of course, is the ultimate small business. At mid-career this is, perhaps for the first time, a viable option. The rules are maddeningly simple and incredibly difficult. Go in a direction you know a great deal about. Plan on everything taking ten times as long as projected. Make customers the focus of everything. Don't spend money you don't have. Learn to make emotional as well as objective decisions. Understand that there are no absolutes, including these.

So without going into exhaustive detail, big, medium, or small/start-up just about cover it. If you have not by this time in you career worked in all of these types, you now have a rough idea of what to expect in those you have missed.

There is often concern about correct sequencing of the size of the organizations one works for. You can move in almost any sequence and make it work. Start-ups usually come later rather than sooner. Big companies usually come sooner rather than later. Medium seems to work well at all stages and in any sequence. Before you move from one category to another, it is best to take the differences outlined briefly here and explore them in greater depth from both a practical and philosophical perspective. You don't want to uncover surprises after a move. All moves will include some unknowns. The fewer major ones the better.

One factor that is constant throughout all sizes and kinds of organizations is the human element. You should maintain contacts across all sizes of business. You will have the benefit of a multidisciplined network that will give you insights by its diversity alone.

Principles of operation are remarkably similar in all sizes when it comes to fundamentals. What works transfers more easily than is commonly thought. Career opportunities of different types are available in each size category.

If you choose the movement from dependence towards independence, you may move down the size scale to whatever level fits your needs and comfort requirements. The taste of independent operation tends to increase your tolerance for risk in almost direct proportion.

CHAPTER 5

YOUR ADVISORY NETWORK

> **Your objective is to avoid operating in a vacuum.**

> **Your personal advisors can come from almost anywhere except your present place of work.**

Career strategies and the construction of a career mosaic are not solitary pursuits.

What you need is a personal board of directors—a group of people who know you, who are not involved in your everyday life, who can provide advice, leads, ideas, and a career overview from their perspective that you could not develop on your own. It is important that you make a conscious effort to collect some senior-advisor types, and then keep in touch with them on a regular basis. It may only be a note or a letter every few months, or a lunch or after-work meeting once a quarter, but some kind of contact is important. This is a low-cost but high-return investment.

Your objective is to avoid operating in a vacuum, not to develop tunnel vision, not to be so tied up in the day-to-day of your current situation that you fail to see what is happening, or fail to keep a realistic eye on the future.

Your personal advisors can come from almost anywhere except your present place of work. It is always best to keep your planning/advisory process separate in every way from your daily operations.

Mixing the two is a double-negative. First, any on-the-job advice will of necessity have some kind of bias, and second, as mentioned, confidentiality is just about impossible to maintain in your workplace.

One advantage of a couple of early career moves is that everyone that you couldn't confide in as a coworker, now becomes available as a sounding board. Very often senior people will have made moves of their own and are thus twice removed and of even greater value.

If you stop and think for a few minutes just who you know, who you respect, and who you would feel comfortable accepting advice from, you should be able to come up with a list of at least five or six people.

Developing a detached outside advisory group is perhaps the single most important career strategy. It provides a means of evaluating all other strategies. Advisors often give you quick answers that cut through what you may feel are insoluble blocks. What seem like highly complex career decisions are just simple problems to people who have been there before you.

> **Developing a detached outside advisory group is perhaps the single most important career strategy. It provides a means of evaluating all other strategies.**

JOINING THE PROS

Although professional organizations are time-consuming, they are worth their weight in gold for the contacts and information they provide. Isolation and single-faceted views can only be avoided by paying the price of professional contacts.

Although the speakers and programs these groups attract will be of some value, it's the stories and strategies shared by fellow members that are the greatest source of career-planning data. Schedule several professional organization commitments and then drop out of those which are least productive.

When you first join a group you have the most to gain if you became an active member. If that means joining committees, going to extra meetings or whatever, that is how you get maximum return. As you gain some seniority, you become a learning resource for junior members coming in. Don't discount this curve as you begin to give back more than you seem to be getting out. Hopefully, you will have identified some fellow members who will become worthwhile peer associates, and perhaps, if you are lucky, you will find a senior mentor as well.

HOW ADVISORS WORK

One junior professional met the president of a small company while involved in church work. The two of them became casual friends. A natural advisory relationship developed. When a career move was in progress for the junior person, a brief touch-base luncheon turned into a practice contract negotiating session. Three weeks later when the real terms of employment were actually on the table, the official meeting seemed like a reenactment of the practice exercise. Knowing in advance what he was going for and, indeed, what in all likelihood was actually negotiable, gave the junior manager a tremendous advantage. The meeting was friendly, and because the outfit was seriously interested, the terms came easily.

Without the earlier run-through, the junior manager wouldn't have known what direction to go in. As an interesting aside, the senior advisor let slip in the run-through conversation that he thought the move was a good one, but that it would not be permanent because the fit of the individual with the organization was too much of a personality reach. He proved to be right, as five years later they had a similar luncheon meeting to work out how best to gain maximum separation terms.

Your group of informal advisors can be a constant while situations shift and develop over the years. In times of fast-moving success, and in times of shifting sands, an uninvolved third party is the best source to help bring reality to light.

> **In times of fast-moving success, and in times of shifting sands, an uninvolved third party is the best source to help bring reality to light.**

A manager was serving as an officer of a local professional organization. The group's president wanted to do a first-class job during his term in office and asked the manager for considerable extra effort. Again, the relationship developed into a professional friendship. Years later, when the manager was between jobs, the president he had served so well set up a lifesaving consulting assignment with several divisions of his company. He did it without being asked. It was good business for both parties.

Every now and then an opportunity presents itself for you to do a favor for those you turn to for advice, but for the most part, these are almost always one-way relationships. The only way you can indirectly respond is by making yourself available to give people junior to you an occasional helping hand.

This system is not, of course, entirely altruistic. There is a certain satisfaction in helping others, and it is more of a compliment than many think to be asked for advice. You don't use people in these relationships, but you can't be shy about seeking them out and keeping them informed.

RESPONSE RULES

You must follow up on the contacts given or advice offered. Reporting back on results or lack of results is part of the process. The loop must be closed on each advisory or networking encounter in order for it to remain available to you in the future. This is where your thank-you note and personal stationery get put to good use. This is the glue that holds all those magic pieces in place.

> **The loop must be closed on each advisory or networking encounter in order for it to remain available to you in the future.**

> **There is far more to peer contact than casual friendships. These people see your world in ways that you cannot.**

We all tend from time to time to get totally immersed in our day-to-day world; oftentimes, we do not maintain the kind of control or direction that is in our best interest. Contact outside our daily peer group at reasonable intervals is a way of evaluating progress and making mid-course corrections. Check your personal files and see how regular your correspondence is. Failure to keep lines of communication open and in working order with senior advisors and professional friends is a major strategic error.

PEER PERSPECTIVE

Ideally, peer contacts should also remain outside your current employment. If you have made a move or two, your "alumni" group is a first-class source for bouncing ideas and situations off people who know your work and your work style. At the same time listen carefully to what they are doing. Try to use their experiences as learning elements in building your own strategies. There is far more to peer contact than casual friendships. These people see your world in ways that you cannot. If you don't ask for their views, you won't get them. All inputs are of value if only to add balance.

As your circle of contacts expands, it will provide inside information on other organizations and industries. Contacts can actually be a source of leads and introductions in potential moves. Peer discussions not only provide an opportunity for you to focus on the present and immediate future but also to articulate just what you are all about. Make time on your schedule for peer give-and-take. Assign it a priority position. You need outside air, outside light, and the free flow of career ideas. Work hard at this segment of your career strategy. It's the easiest to let slide, yet it can be the most pleasant strategy to maintain.

In all cases, people contact will have great career strategic benefits, if you learn to cultivate and keep relationships of value open.

This is a life-long project. You will turn to senior professionals for many years, so think in terms of how best to get maximum return on relationships.

You are in day-to-day contact with a sizable number of peers and juniors. Be careful of inside relationships, but cultivate those that can be of value for career perspectives.

Outside contacts are the life's blood of career information, strategies, and values. They require considerable time. If you do not invest this time in your own behalf, you will greatly limit vital input.

Once you accept the concept that you must do things in your own best interest to manage the ebb and flow of your career, you then must accept the challenge of taking action.

> **Break out of the world of your daily work environment.**

Break out of the world of your daily work environment. Don't let your job responsibilities isolate you from others. Your current assignment must be considered temporary. Your network contacts are permanent. Treat both accordingly. Don't shortchange yourself by misdirected dedication and excessive obligation to duty. Your most important duty is to yourself.

> **Your current assignment must be considered temporary. Your network contacts are permanent.**

MAKING
MOVES

Y ou may have already made some moves either internal or external, domestic or international, or even across an industry or two. You have an idea of what is involved. On occasion in a career, you will even make involuntary moves. Let's hope there aren't too many of those, although they are seemingly unavoidable. One way to provide at least a modicum of career life insurance is to move on a preplanned basis before potentially dangerous unplanned moves develop. Beating someone to the punch is an excellent strategy.

On the up side of the mobility picture, you can generate quantum leaps in both income and opportunity, if you are willing to work constantly at engineering career moves. Some see this as the thrill of the game, others as the price to be paid. Either way, making moves versus being moved is the challenge.

The amount of effort necessary to make a carefully prepared move is considerable. It's not unusual to invest six to ten months in the process of transition. Seldom do situations develop rapidly. One of the most difficult career strategies to maintain involves keeping yourself in the marketplace during good times. The temptation to "settle in" can be suicidal. No move should ever be considered a final move.

Compartmentalizing your professional life so that you are a contributing member of your current organization while developing future career prospects is not a casual undertaking. It's a discipline that if mastered can pay off in the generation of some worthwhile opportunities.

Everything, of course, doesn't happen according to plan, but getting a plan in motion will provide a framework for other elements to materialize.

> No move should ever be considered a final move.

> You should never feel so secure and be so happy that you can't take the time to look and explore.

KEEPING OPTIONS OPEN

Logic tells us that talking to others about potential opportunities when we don't feel the pressure for action is the best possible scenario. Reality tells us that when things are going well (we just received a promotion, a raise, a great review), we move career prospecting far down on the list. We even turn down chances to explore options. You should never feel so secure and be so happy that you can't take the time to look and explore. If the timing is wrong, that's life—but open all doors before you decide to close them (or better still always leave them ajar).

Good career health requires options. Some will come your way and all you need to know is how to handle them. Others must be painstakingly nurtured over months and sometimes years. Gaining career independence means working at developing situations and then making go/no-go decisions when they are ripe for the picking.

Working at a promotion and promoting yourself can be done simultaneously. The problem is that we always put great effort into the former and neglect the latter. A balanced effort is the objective. Look at your daily "to do" list. Are all the items directed at getting ahead internally, or do you have some on there that could support the generation of outside opportunities?

If you are not doing anything on a day-to-day basis for your personal professional growth, then you are not doing anything for yourself long term.

Mid-career mobility, and even just the possibility of generating mobility opportunities, requires hard work. It is satisfying work because you are working for yourself. If you don't want to get backed into some difficult career situations, then begin to think about what you can do to set the foundations for an engineered move. Pick out an idea or two. Meet with some outside professional friends. Then establish a contact. Put something on your list of things to do for this week or this month. Assign that item a priority. Before you can develop career momentum, you must first overcome career inertia with some small but real action.

Step one is allotting sufficient time to be open to contacts. Information, as we discussed, can lead to opportunities. By keeping the contact network alive and well, you open up the possibility of actual opportunities. Yet, it's all too easy to close down this invaluable source by reducing or eliminating the time allotted. Failure to attend outside professional events or to maintain outside contacts serves the same negative purpose.

> **Working at a promotion and promoting yourself can be done simultaneously.**

> **Before you can develop career momentum, you must first overcome career inertia.**

> **A career mobility strategy cannot be focused on finding a safe, secure place to settle into.**

> **There is always the possibility that each career move will be your last, but the laws of probability dictate against this.**

CHANGE IS CONSTANT

Conventional wisdom says that most career moves should be made early, that as our judgment and view of ourselves matures, we will settle into our life's work. That wisdom discounts one major factor: the constant motion of the marketplace and fluctuating business trends.

A career mobility strategy cannot be focused on finding a safe, secure place to settle into. First, there is no such place. Second, you will lose your competitive edge to make a contribution, and thus much of your market value, by discounting the dynamics of opportunity.

Yes, there is always the possibility that each career move will be your last, but the laws of probability dictate against this. It is far wiser to plan on potential mobility than to attempt to hang on to one situation beyond its useful career life.

No one knows how many moves will be made. All that is certain is that some will be necessary. The minimum will be your initial entry into the workplace which is behind you, and a retirement transition which is ahead of you. The maximum is a hard estimate to make, but a reasonable rule of thumb indicates that you will move or be moved with some kind of career change every two and one-half to three years. If you are behind this figure at present you may catch up, or if you are ahead of these numbers you may slow down, but by facing the facts of mobility and change you can be better prepared to deal with them.

You must be a student of two constantly moving dynamics. First, what is the internal situation? What is really happening to both you and your organization? Second, what is the outside situation? What opportunities are under development that could be converted into a potential positive career move?

If the internal situation seems favorable (and it can change overnight), you can then merely cultivate outside targets of opportunity. If the internal situation has some dark clouds, you had better not just wish for brighter days. Your act should be in gear on the outside, getting yourself favorably positioned for the contacts and meetings that, under the best circumstances, will extend out over several months. Engineering a move is time-consuming, even when everything goes perfectly.

THE TIME FACTOR

One company had been acquired by its largest competitor, and although dual operations were under way in the marketplace, conflicts were inevitable. It was only a question of time until axes began to fall.

After talking to some people in the industry, a thirty-five-year-old professional, who had made a couple of internal career moves, decided that his head would be on the block sooner or later. He was at the top of his field for this particular kind of business and, therefore, would do better if he could transfer his skills across industry lines. His hope was that he could stay geographically fixed, and since he was in range of a major metropolitan area, this was a reasonable objective.

As most junior people will do, he scanned the classified ads with little result. Then, he happened upon the name of a consultant he knew who was serving as the respondent to a semi-blind ad for a staff assignment that fit his background. A phone call produced all the necessary data, and he decided to throw his hat in the ring.

He set up a meeting with his friend to see what the search procedure involved and to develop a strategy for becoming one of the top contenders to be passed on to the client company executive.

Everything went exactly as planned. Meeting followed meeting and one by one the competition was eliminated and an offer was made.

The total process from the first phone call until he was on the payroll took over eight months. No one ever had any negative impressions, everything worked out in proper sequence; it's just that all the necessary interviews, meetings, negotiations, decision points had to proceed according to a schedule. That schedule belonged to the agenda of the vice president who was making the hire and, of course, his boss and several others also had to be fed into the mix. All of those steps added up to the eight months. This was not an excessive time for this type of deliberate and relatively conservative big company management team.

This may be the outside time-frame for a favorable move, but it was the real time-frame for an actual move. You must deal with the reality of extended efforts even under the most favorable circumstances.

Things take time to develop properly. They can't easily be rushed. They usually can't be rushed at all. The organization or person making the decision will work on his or her or its own schedule regardless of your needs.

Accepting this fact is just one more reason for not only early action but constant action.

> **Things take time to develop properly. They can't easily be rushed. They usually can't be rushed at all.**

TAKING ACTION

It is most unlikely that you will be hit by lightning unless you spend a great deal of time standing out in rain storms. People like to say things like "and then a friend of mine called and I joined the ABC Company." This kind of remark is used to describe the eight-month type transition just recounted, so don't be misled by the seeming ease and flow of the events. Reality is a lot different than the memory of what transpired.

One of the reasons that people stay in situations much longer than common sense would dictate is the degree of difficulty involved in making a move. Seldom is a position so desperate that it can't be endured for a little while longer in the hope that something will change—or so we tell ourselves.

Unfortunately, the only changes you can count on are those changes you make for yourself. If you set up a move, you can then, and only then, be assured that your situation will be resolved and you will be off to a fresh start.

> **Internal mobility does not accomplish what outside mobility does for your growth.**

> **The only changes you can count on are those changes you make for yourself.**

INTERNAL VS. EXTERNAL MOVES

A major benefit of any outside move is the opportunity to come in at your current level of skill and expertise without any negative background. The slate is clean. You have zero negative history. Everyone doing a job has things go wrong now and then. Human nature being what it is, some people have a long memory for keeping those little glitches "on call" forever.

Mobility is usually a positive in building skills and perspectives in your career field, but internal mobility does not accomplish what outside mobility does for your growth. In some large companies there is a practice of rotational assignments, not only for junior, but mid-level and even some senior managers. The belief is that management develops by exposure and mobility within the corporation. The major benefit of this process seems to be a strengthening of the character of the spouses who have to manage all the logistics of the required geographic moves. What limits the results in management development is that in each new assignment and each new relationship, everyone is still working from the same book. Internal uniformity provides little in the way of variation in style, or creativity, or methods of operation. The learning curve is slight at best.

Ironically, if someone held nine different internal assignments in six years and had made four geographic moves, no one would call that person a job-hopper or unstable. To the contrary, that person was on a "fast track."

If you did the same thing on the outside by moving from one opportunity to another with different organizations, you would be accused of being a high-risk hire. In reality, you would have developed a background that would make you a highly seasoned top professional.

The chance to make quantum leaps in income is a major factor in pursuing a career strategy of external mobility. Promoting yourself, versus waiting for all the stars and planets to be in alignment so that you are promoted by someone else, must be the method of choice.

> **The chance to make quantum leaps in income is a major factor in pursuing a career strategy of external mobility.**

Making two or three mid-career moves seems to require a special type of person with great confidence, personal marketing skills, and an extra measure of courage. You may not see yourself in those terms. But why not? You only have to be fired once in mid-career to discover that, as painful as the process is, you have all of the depth and courage necessary to make a profitable move.

SHAPING YOUR CAREER

There is no need to stay on the move indefinitely. If at any point you have hit a gold-plated opportunity, you can stick with it on into the sunset. The problem comes when we *hope* that those opportunities will somehow materialize out of the woodwork in our present situations.

They usually don't. Just the process of engineering your own career progress builds strength in itself. You review who you are, you develop a reasonable opportunity, and then you sell yourself into it at a worthwhile monetary increase. If you make a mistake, you at least know that you have the ability to engineer another move that may land you in a more favorable environment.

Each move expands your circle of professional contacts. Each move carries with it the opportunity for great potential gain. Each move opens up a new challenge that may uncover a strength you didn't know you had. Each move gives you the power to determine exactly how long you will stay with a negative situation.

CHAPTER 7

AVOIDING THE RESUME TRAP

> The resume is by far the most negative and personally dangerous document you will ever write.

> "The MBA will look good on the resume." Zap! Sixty-thousand dollars and three to six years later you have added three uppercase letters at a cost per letter of heaven knows what in time and treasure.

> To acquire an advanced degree at mid-career is a marginal endeavor at best.

 omewhere in the development of the business lexicon the phrase, "getting your resume up-to-date", became a euphemism for preparing for an outside career move.

The resume and its creation has established a life of its own. It is by far the most negative and personally dangerous document you will ever write. Its primary function is to provide a basis for screening people out of consideration for jobs.

So many people make career judgments based upon how the moves will appear on a resume; if it were not such a serious and widespread practice, this approach would be comical.

"The MBA will look good on the resume." Zap! Sixty-thousand dollars and three to six years later you have added three uppercase letters at a cost of heaven knows what in time and treasure. To acquire an advanced degree at mid-career is a marginal endeavor at best. For the most part, mid-career professional experience will have far exceeded whatever is being taught in a degree program from a practical or usable standpoint.

Staying with an untenable job situation for an extra year so that a "resume respectable" interval is created is another strategy that is all too common. What a waste of one's time, life, and potential. Get it over with and get on with it.

Many books, articles, and cases have been written to prove that excellent career progress can be made without the use of a resume. Why would you ever want to make any decision based upon how it would effect a document that can easily be done without?

Readjust your thinking and do away with all strategies and actions that are designed to enhance a resume.

You don't want to look good on paper. You want to be good in reality. There are worlds of difference between the two. You want to do things that produce results, not things that just result in documentation of some subjective idealized process.

> **Readjust your thinking and do away with all strategies and judgment that are designed to enhance a resume.**

> **You don't want to look good on paper. You want to be good in reality.**

DO WHAT'S RIGHT FOR YOU

One manager stuck with a single assignment for five years so that he could continue to work for a gifted vice president. It was the finest development assignment of his career, and extending it allowed him to learn enough to increase his future value far more than if he had opted to move at the end of two or three years in order to show ideal career progress for his resume.

Another mid-career manager spent several months time in meetings and interviews engineering a move to IBM. At the end of the first day on the job, he knew he had made a mistake. He had the courage to resign at the end of the first week. Imagine how that would look on a resume. He didn't care. He knew what was right for him, or in this case what was wrong, and he proceeded to get on with his life rather than hang in for appearance's sake.

Three or four quick or erratic career moves in succession are not a very good idea in principle. They may require a conservative steady assignment just to rebuild your self-image and to feel good about making a meaningful contribution. How successive moves will appear on a resume should not have any influence on learning how and when to cut your losses and move on.

Organizations that place undue emphasis on paper backgrounds get what they deserve. They get paper people who are heavy on credentials and light on ability to do much beyond seeking the next paper goal.

Keeping your contact file up-to-date, increasing your outside exposure, following up referrals and leads should be the emphasis for getting yourself on the go. Playing paper games is an exercise in futility.

> **How successive moves will appear on a resume should not have any influence on learning how and when to cut your losses and move on.**

> **Organizations that place undue emphasis on paper backgrounds get what they deserve.**

> **More career opportunities have been lost because of rejected resumes than for any other single cause.**

RESUMES: DANGEROUS TO YOUR CAREER HEALTH

The second euphemism in business involving the resume is the idea that when someone says "send me a resume", they actually mean they will do something positive or of value for you.

When you hear or read "send me a resume"—beware! It means you are being asked to supply documentation of a highly detailed nature for some kind of subjective evaluation against unknown criteria, often by someone you don't know and who usually doesn't know you. Of all the things that can result from this process, the probability of any of them being positive is remote at best. More career opportunities have been lost because of rejected resumes than for any other single cause. Why would you fashion the club with which you are to be beaten?

If you don't have a resume, then you can't send one to anyone. Preparing a resume should be the last step in becoming mobile, not the first. If after all kinds of meetings, exchanges of ideas, outlining of specific criteria, and general good feelings of compatibility, it is necessary to provide a resume or written document to technically close a loop in a career move, then tailor a special first edition for this single set of circumstances.

Not having a current resume will keep you out of the quick response trap. If for some reason you must stick your head in the lion's mouth, you will at least be forced to make the move slowly with individual attention, instead of a reflex action which may result in instant career decapitation.

Resumes are used to screen out.

Resumes are either filed or piled. In one, they disappear forever; in the other, they are sorted out against their paper competitors.

If some kind of documentation is appropriate, a carefully crafted personal letter is always the instrument of choice over any kind of a resume. The strategy to follow is to seek an undocumented face-to-face casual meeting in order to get acquainted. You want to avoid being screened out on paper or getting yourself involved in a screening interview. Being screened out by the key decision maker is one thing, but being screened out for some background anomaly, or the failure to fit some hypothetical profile, is a truly ignominious strategic career defeat. Resumes are used to screen out. They are scanned, not read. They are used to uncover subjective "red flags" and "knockout" factors. Ironically, those with the most unusual backgrounds, with the most to offer at mid-life, are the most susceptible to screen out.

Resumes are either filed or piled. In one, they disappear forever; in the other, they are sorted out against their paper competitors. Any professional who gets into this mess probably deserves the consequences.

You don't want an evaluation based on paper documentation as the lead element in a career move. First of all, you want an early two-way information exchange. You want some first hand face-to-face data upon which to make your judgments as to whether to proceed or not.

You want a valid and as close to an equal exchange as possible. Would you turn down a meeting in favor of a copy of an annual report?

> **There is no such thing as a high-level executive resume. One eliminates the other.**

> **Your objective in any initial written contact is never to be considered directly for a position.**

Of course not. You want to gain an overall impression. You want to use all of your senses. You want to get a feel for the people. Paper, either yours or theirs, can't do that.

If you can find no other way to make a contact other than by mail, then write a letter of interest on your own high quality stationery, addressed to the key person, requesting a brief meeting. State as few reasons or qualifications as possible. Hit one hard. Make it your strongest point and be sure it is relative to whatever you know about the situation. Your objective in any initial written contact is never to be considered directly for a position. It should always be to gain a face-to-face meeting to exchange preliminary information and to gather impressions.

Always the strategy must be to make the resume the superfluous document that it ought to be. Comment: "Let me pass along your resume to Joe." Reply: "I've heard a lot about him. How about setting up a get-acquainted meeting. I'd like to meet him. I have a couple of questions I'd like to ask." or, "Why not just tell Joe I will be in touch? I will write him a note and copy you."

Better that you lose an opportunity while trying to convert it to a favorable encounter than you go down the drain as a piece of waste paper.

By mid-career you should have passed most of the lower-level moves that are most susceptible to resume collection and evaluation. There is no such thing as a high-level executive resume. One eliminates the other.

Social contacts, casual meetings and/or personal referrals all operate well above the paper-trap league. To make or to seek solid career moves from mid-career on, you must not only learn to avoid the paper games but to operate comfortably above and beyond these lower-level screening devices.

One final note of caution. You may agree totally with all of these ideas and then have someone do a resume for you without your ever knowing it. This can happen when you work with third-party agents in the employment industry. They love the idea of working with paper. They think spec sheets are the way to go. They often earn their fees on their ability to produce a person that fits exactly into a hypothetical profile. Matching specifications is their stock in trade. Let's talk about them next.

CHAPTER 8

THE EMPLOYMENT INDUSTRY: HEADHUNTERS TO EXECUTIVE SEARCH

> **Put yourself in their position for a few minutes. They are client driven—and you are not the client.**

In looking at where you might be going and some of the means available to you to get there, you can't discount the potential value of the people who have made it their careers (at least temporarily) to match talent to needs.

The employment industry covers everything from prestigious executive search firms to the body-moving mass employment outfits to outplacement organizations working the other end of the tunnel. (Career counseling will be addressed separately in chapter 9, Love for Sale.) With all its various segments, this industry works more closely to the supply-and-demand curves than do many other industries.

Put yourself in their position for a few minutes. They are client driven—and you are not the client. They are paid by those organizations that hire them to find people, or in the case of outplacement, to dump them. In times of industry downturns, they sell outplacement services, so they go in whatever direction the client winds blow. They often work with personnel or employment people within the client organization. Some even work directly with line managers and, in the case of executive search companies, they often deal at the highest levels.

Those in the employment industry are aware of the stratification of their business. Naturally they will gravitate towards the high end when discussing what they do. A straight employment agency that pushes paper, moves bodies, and/or operates a telephone boiler room sales group, will often say it is in the executive search business. Or it will report that it does "contingency search work," meaning that if it can sell someone to a client, it will get paid.

The quality of these operations and the quality of the people in them are all over the lot. What you must keep in mind is that almost everyone in this business works on commission, paid by the client on some kind of a percentage-of-income formula. The exception to this process is a retainer-plus-expenses search assignment where the search firm is paid even if the client company rejects the candidates submitted. But that's for big time top management slots only.

WHERE YOU FIT IN

It is safe to say that the vast majority of employment industry contacts you will have at mid-career will be with commission sales representatives. Their priorities must lie first with themselves and the generation of their income, secondly with the well-being of their clients, and lastly with you whom they will use as best they can for the satisfaction of the first two. This doesn't mean the system doesn't work; it does. It's just that it works according to priorities, and if you understand those priorities, you will be better able to deal with the reality of each opportunity.

In all cases you are the product. Unlike the contact network, industry grapevine, professional association relationship process, the employment industry operates on packaging and listed ingredients. They need specifications. They work against profiles. They love "name" brands. They are selling, and they want to be able to describe their products in terms that will be meaningful to their customers. Credentials in this selling process are important. This is where the advanced degree from the name school, the big company background (preferably from one that does TV advertising and is a household name), are used to gain client attention.

> **Employment industry priorities must lie first with themselves and the generation of their income, secondly with the well-being of their clients, and lastly with you whom they will use as best they can for the satisfaction of the first two.**

> **The employment industry operates on packaging and listed ingredients.**

> **They want standard type-one plain vanilla.**

BLAND, BUT BEAUTIFUL

The fact that you are six feet tall (either male or female) is important, as if you could do something about it or it made any difference in your value. Your cosmetic appearance counts heavily in this process. Not just being neat and well-dressed, but the big smile, good looks and athletic body are all important packaging features. Having brains and ability are also a nice add-on feature, but the industry operates first and foremost on the externals.

They need a product that makes an impression. They want all the "right" features and benefits for their clients. They don't want to have to explain variations. They want standard type-one plain vanilla. They want textbook career patterns. They want gold-plated, airtight resumes. They want to deliver what looks good, feels good, and what gives everyone the impression they are dealing with top quality merchandise.

If all this sounds inhuman, mercenary or superficial, you can begin to understand where the industry terms "flesh peddler" and "body snatcher" have come from. It's not that there are not many skilled professionals of high integrity working in the employment industry. It's just that the overall structure has more faults than strengths, and in some cases it tends to run counter to the best interests of those who get involved with it.

The main point to keep in mind is that the employment industry operates for the benefit of someone other than you. It operates on standard cosmetic "name" brand recognition, credentials/background and profile criteria. It is effective for only a small percentage of people seeking opportunity and advancement in their careers, even though it services a large market segment as far as clients are concerned. It offers quick fixes to people's needs, and there will always be managers and industries that will buy those services.

BETTER COMPANIES, BETTER METHODS

Finding and hiring high quality people is a primary management responsibility in every discipline. It should not be delegated to outside vendors except in extraordinary cases, and those causes and cases should be eliminated as a matter of good management practice at the earliest possible date.

Incoming quality control of people is a function of highest priority for all concerned. Those organizations that approach this task carefully and professionally are for the most part better places to work than those that relegate people selection to an "as needed" basis, or who feel that it can be a service purchased from the outside. Well-managed companies will not rule out candidates supplied from the employment industry, but they will use them only as supplements to the continuous prospecting process they maintain as a regular part of their day-to-day operations.

If, by the way, you happen to have all of the things necessary to become a first-class product for the employment industry to sell, it ought to occur to you that you could market yourself just as well or better by taking yourself through the network contact processes we have already discussed. If you look good through one channel, you look even better through the other. If, on the other hand, you are not one of the beautiful people with the test pattern background, you can begin to see where the employment industry will not be quite as valuable to you as it might be. Don't write it off, but understand why it won't be the answer to your prayers. So many people feel that if they just put their destiny in the hands of some personnel agency their future will be assured. Your career progress must be considered a high priority do-it-yourself project. It can't be done for you or to you. You must accept responsibility for who you are and where you are going as well as how you are going to get there. You will always be the one best qualified to put together the pieces of your career mosaic.

> **Your career progress must be considered a high priority do-it-yourself project. It can't be done for you or to you.**

BEST
STRATEGIES

What can the non-perfect person do with all these various kinds of people brokers? The answer is add them to your contact network, if the opportunity presents itself. Don't seek them out, but don't turn them off either. Don't put them down. Treat them like human beings and give them the benefit of the doubt. As mentioned, with an industry not known for its quality, there are some exceptions. You would like to know a few of these exceptional industry professionals if possible, so you are going to have to pay the price necessary to sift through the also-rans.

The industry works by phone for the most part, so being alert to phone contacts is important. If you are on the hiring end in your current organizaiton, not necessarily in personnel but in a growth area, and you are therefore targeted as a potential client by outside sales reps, by all means listen to their story. Give them the straight scoop on what is going on in your department or company and, if appropriate, talk to a candidate or two of theirs in order to gauge the credibility of your contact. In short, establish a business relationship, if at all possible. It's good business for whomever you work, and it is of course good business for you now and in the future.

What you are looking for is a rep who either has been in the business for a while, or who appears likely to remain in the industry. These are good people to trade names and information with. These exchanges are in every way ethical and a normal part of keeping track of what is going on and who is doing what and where.

Because agencies either specialize in specific disciplines or industries, and individual sales representatives work in areas where they can use the same contacts and people over and over again, it's not hard to get a complete picture of what is going on in your field. Use this information relative to all of your other sources of data—trade publications, professional association contacts, civic organizations, and others you've selected to keep current with.

Building contacts as a buyer or potential client in the employment industry results in the possibility of your becoming a potential product for sale by your vendor. Stay open to all of these overtures, but do so with caution, even with those vendors you know. You don't want to end up as one of their direct mail spec sheets, even if your name isn't listed directly.

You want to keep the lines of communication open. The sales rep is looking for a bonus or commission, so on the off chance that you may make a move, it is in his or her best interest to help the situation along. It's always best to do a great deal of shopping around before you buy anything. It is even better to shop when you don't need anything. We all know enough not to go to the grocery store when we are hungry. We all know the benefits of working from a shopping list. It's amazing how many people make career moves because they just happen to be contacted or asked. There is nothing wrong with taking an unexpected opportunity, but being in the hunt part time all the time is the strategy to follow rather than following impulse-buying tendencies. So few people think about managing their own careers, either internally or externally, that they lose the skills, or fail to develop the skills, to manage career information as it presents itself.

> **Until you have an offer there is really nothing to say no to. Up until that point it is just a dance.**

DANCE TO YOUR OWN BEAT

Whenever anything begins to develop through a personnel sales rep contact, the general rule is to follow the lead one step beyond where you have made a screen-out judgment. The benefit in doing this will be that you will add to your contact/informational data bank. You will gain the tactical experience of going the additional steps necessary to generate a potential opportunity, or in some cases an actual offer. Until you have an offer there is really nothing to say no to. Up until that point it is just a dance. Nothing wrong with career dancing. It's good for your health. Don't feel badly about wasting the time and effort of a personnel industry sales rep if you're not serious about a move at the present time. It's all a part of the business. They get enough sales in impulse career moves to support extended work with more savvy professionals. Besides, there is always the outside chance that something will click and that makes things worthwhile for all concerned.

If, because of your professional visibility you get contacts from outside recruiters, you should develop the appropriate responses.

The standard rule when the call comes is not to say yes or no, always say maybe. Learn to discipline yourself to make explorations for possible future needs, so you will have the resources available when you decide to put a career mobility strategy into action. You don't have to lead people on. You can accurately describe your situation as stable, but open to possibilities. Find out what the next step is and see what it will take to get there. Going down the path many times for practice will pay off when you decide to do it for real. More than one practice exercise has turned up either an immediate opportunity or a solid professional contact that proved to be of great future value.

> Going down the
> path many times
> for practice will
> pay off when
> you decide to do
> it for real.

Opportunities will be presented in a once-in-a-life-time framework when you are dealing with the employment industry. Scale that back immediately.

NOTHING IS FOREVER

Opportunities will be presented in a once-in-a-life-time framework when you are dealing with the employment industry. Scale that back immediately. It is highly unlikely that each move you will make will be for life. Focus on short term or near term; that will be more realistic than long term in most cases. At mid-career you have more to sell than you might think, and therefore you might have more power in negotiations than you ever have had in the past. Don't discount the value of someone approaching you. It could be worth a twenty or thirty percent income jump over and above what a position might be worth if you were going after it, instead of the other way around.

Being too eager, responding with a preprinted resume, giving out organizational information or the names of potential contacts can be very, very expensive errors in judgment. At mid-career you should learn to be measured in your responses to contacts from the employment industry. Knowing who they come from, what they do for a living, and where their priorities must lie will allow you to make them a part of your career strategy but only on your own terms. Depending upon how you look to them superficially may determine how much use you can make of them for your own benefit.

There is no need to try to appear to be something you are not just to attempt to tune into this source. Your standard personal marketing strategies must be primary anyway. It is far better to invest your efforts in your personal marketing strategies than build frustrations trying to deal with an industry whose methods of operation lack objective validity in favor of expediency.

Either way, take things on your own terms. Do those things that are in your own professional best interest. Understand how the system works, and work that part of the system where you have the greatest strengths. Being in any way outside the mainstream should not cause you to do everything you can to get on the inside track. It should instead cause you to determine how best to proceed in your present environment and to be realistic in looking at the vast number of options, rather than focusing on what appears to be or is reported to be the ideal pattern or path.

> **Understand how the system works, and work that part of the system where you have the greatest strengths.**

CHAPTER 9

CAREER-COUNSELING SERVICES: LOVE FOR SALE

What career counseling does is put people through a process of "services" which conventional wisdom indicates will help a person find and get a better job. This conventional wisdom is flawed.

The false bottom in the industry is that it does not and cannot provide new opportunities.

Y ou are not alone. Senior contacts in your field, peer professionals from past companies, trusted friends all can provide counsel and help you formulate and evaluate career strategies. You must, however, accept the responsibility of doing the hard work of tapping into these groups yourself. You must build skills. You must construct and maintain a network. You must become comfortable with the process of seeking and giving support over a long period of time.

FLAWED
WISDOM

Because this challenge is not an easy one, people search for alternatives. Many individuals simply do not understand how the system works; they are prime candidates to respond to the promise of career-counseling advertisements. They don't have either the confidence or the knowledge to go it alone. They know that their present situation isn't good and they don't see a way out. They look through the classifieds and perhaps respond to a few ads. Then they find what appears to be the answer to their prayers.

These are big ads, often in the front of the classified section of the newspaper. They are headed "Career Services." They offer help (and hope). They state clearly that they are not employment services. They state more clearly that they offer career assistance. The logic of not being able to handle things alone and therefore seeking professional assistance seems sensible and straightforward. In fact, the career counseling industry has built its business on this premise. The false bottom in the industry is, of course, that it does not and cannot provide new opportunities. It cannot and does not set people up with contacts. It cannot and does not do the hard work necessary for any kind of a career move. What career counseling does is put people through a process of "services" which conventional wisdom indicates will help a person find and get a better job. This conventional wisdom is flawed.

Constructing a resume, printing it on expensive paper, and mailing it with a professionally prepared cover letter won't produce opportunity. Being tested and interviewed by a "professional" counselor doesn't give you a single contact. (The counselor has read a book on careers—not this one—and will take you through the chapters. It's a very expensive way of reading a book.)

Gaining access to a vast data bank may seem worthwhile until you discover that the career-counseling company has either duplicated a free list or rented a list that is generally available to the public from directories or at a public library. The "services" then amount to: an evaluation meeting and report, resume and cover-letter writing, a direct mail program, perhaps some videotape interview role-playing, and, last but not least, the investment of a considerable amount of cash to support the overhead and profit structure of the counseling business.

A NO-WIN SITUATION

Within this industry there are dedicated professionals who do provide the support and direction that some people cannot generate for themselves. Unfortunately, these few worthwhile individuals are impossible to identify, because, before you can even meet them, you must sign a contract and make the payment of a fee.

One tip-off factor that will indicate the nature of the career-counseling process is the absolute attention to the legal detail of the relationship you contract for. A five- or six-page carefully worded list of services with a guarantee that these services will be delivered is presented for signature. These contracts have been legally tested many, many times and are binding documents. You can cancel them under most laws only within three days of signing them. In the case of the career-counseling business, little or no service has been rendered in that time period. Dissatisfaction usually takes several weeks or months to set in.

It is an unfortunate fact that many people who are between jobs spend whatever money they have or can borrow on these programs in the desperate hope of getting a job. An up-front payment of $2500 to $5000 is not uncommon. Credit cards are accepted and the idea of "investing" in yourself is a major part of the sales presentation. The sales person you talk with works on a ten to twenty percent commission plan, and his or her well-being depends upon getting your cash on the table by the end of your first meeting. They can tell you truthfully that you look to them to be worth more than you are being paid and that there are opportunities for people like you to do much better. It is difficult to disagree with these ideas. They are probably correct. What to do about the situation is what is at issue. Buying thousands of dollars in seemingly related "services" isn't a very cost-effective answer.

DO-IT-YOURSELF

The entire focus of your career strategy must be people-oriented, not process-oriented. One may seem to lead to the other, but the connection is tenuous at best. Inwardly directed processes of resume writing, direct mailings (about you) and "counseling" (of you) are 180 degrees out of phase with the outwardly focused steps needed to develop opportunities. You have to meet insiders who know what is going on in their business or industry. You have to develop specific information from reliable personal sources rather than rely on general information and public sources.

Skills cannot be developed in front of a video camera. They must be developed in repeated actual use. Seeing yourself by means of videotape isn't a bad

> **The entire focus of your career strategy must be people-oriented, not process-oriented.**

> **If you could videotape an ideal meeting you would discover that you would have said or done very little. Good contact meetings are one-sided affairs— theirs!**

idea. It's just that paying thousands of dollars to do so isn't very smart. You can buy a home video camera dirt cheap. You can borrow a friend's outfit. You can go to your local high school and ask to use public equipment. (Students will be happy to tape you.) What you will learn will be to sit up straight, dress conservatively, and to hold solid eye contact. When you meet with people it is important to ask them good questions and listen to their answers. You don't need video role-playing skills for that. Not only can you and should you work from a written list of questions, but you can put notes in the margins on posture, eye contact, and listening, as well. If you could videotape an ideal meeting you would discover that you would have said or done very little. The less you do the better. Good contact meetings are one-sided affairs—theirs! You need to develop skills to make them so, but it's real life practice that increases confidence and skill.

A danger in videotape play-acting is that whether you want to or not, you will compare yourself against the broadcast standards of the evening news. That is not a realistic comparison. A real meeting or two with an actual contact and your own self-evaluation against your strategy are far better skill-building techniques than using video role-play.

BETTER AVAILABLE RESOURCES

Paying for something that is available for free has been the basis of some very old professions. They do serve a market. The question is do you want to be a part of that market?

Real career strategies and ideas are as inexpensive as this book. Those people necessary to implement them are all around you. One pleasant surprise is how accessible and helpful good solid people can be.

The career-counseling industry works against a real need. They have no advertised competition. Seminars and workshops run on a scheduled calendar basis by universities and public seminar companies are promoted quietly to limited audiences, usually through direct mail or alumni lists. While they also serve the real need of providing insight and support, they are one time events and are not nearly as highly visible in the marketplace as are the specialized counseling firms. *National Business Employment Weekly* lists a monthly schedule of career workshops and events by region. That publication, which comes out each Sunday, is an excellent investment, both for this schedule of events and its general career-oriented editorial content.

If you are a college graduate, you may discover that your university has an alumni career director who may be of help. At the very least, alumni lists or directories are available which may provide a contact name or two from which to begin a referral chain.

Any professional typing service can do correspondence. If you have done the face-to-face contact work first, there is no need to attempt to craft a super documented package of cover letters, broadcast mailers, and resumes. The most important correspondence you will have to deal with will always be your personal thank-you notes.

You certainly don't need professional help in preparing a one paragraph, three or four sentence, personal note. The only technique you must master is to make your notes conversational and stay away from standard sentences and phrases. A reference to a

Everything that is sold by the career-counseling industry for thousands of dollars can be purchased on an as-needed basis for under a hundred dollars.

specific comment or observation is all that is necessary to make your follow up a custom versus a form response.

Everything that is sold by the career-counseling industry for thousands of dollars can be purchased on an as-needed basis for under a hundred dollars. The whole process of developing career strategies is now becoming a part of the professional skill package that more and more people are equipping themselves with as they progress along their varied paths. And that is very good news.

The do-it-yourself approach is the only one that assures that you will get the results you go after. Putting the pieces of a career mosaic together is far too personal a task to place in the hands of others. You can develop information from hundreds of sources, you can have access to large numbers of people—all for just the asking. The purchase of a prepackaged set of services that seem to be somehow related to career progression is a questionable strategy at best and a demoralizing and expensive experience at worst.

> **Putting the pieces of a career mosaic together is far too personal a task to place in the hands of others.**

IT TAKES TIME

If the ads tempt you, make a call to the local Better Business Bureau. If you find nothing there, ask the firm for a list of satisfied clients.

Even some of the better known names in the career-counseling field that have been around for many years have been in and out of litigation and bankruptcy a number of times. The high-rise addresses and the

> **Career management means staying ahead of events.**

successful looking offices and sales people are just overhead that must be paid for by customers like you. If there were an easy way, a way to purchase effective career assistance, it would be a giant and successful industry. In reality, it can't be purchased. The time periods you must work through far exceed the economics of a continued paid professional relationship. Career strategies must be worked at over months and years, not days and weeks. Even when you are "self-employed" between jobs, you will have to work full time for yourself for many months getting the next career piece to drop into place. Even company-funded outplacement services provide little more than minimal office services during these extended periods of dislocation.

Being responsible for what you are doing, where you are going, and how you are going to get there is a challenging personal responsibility which cannot be delegated.

Simple things like returning phone calls, maintaining highly diversified contacts, keeping a balanced lifestyle, listening to or reading about the career strategies of others are all part of the on-going process. It takes tremendous career discipline to do the things every day that will eventually become the tools needed to take advantage of opportunities in good times and to get back on track or select new tracks in bad times. Career management means staying ahead of events. Remedial management is sometimes necessary but it is not the kind of thing you want to rely upon.

If you will read one business book a quarter about your field, about how others have progressed (biographies), about how the system works, you will close any perceived knowledge gap between you and the career-counseling industry. If you will broaden and expand your circle of contacts outside of your present work environment, you will have all the support resources you will need at just the cost of your time. If you will take an objective look at where you are and what you are doing on a continuing basis so you do not lose sight of the outside world, and will share that view with others who are not part of your environment, you will never end up signing a multipage contract and paying out thousands of dollars for help that in reality can't be purchased.

CHAPTER 10

CONGRATU-LATIONS: YOU'RE FIRED!

A moving target is difficult to hit.

Instant independence brings with it the stark reality of having to do all at once the things you should have been doing over an extended period of time.

The human need for security is basic. Unfortunately, the idea that organizations provide security is almost as deep-seated.

The biggest advantage of a career strategy based on self-determination and mobility is that you can usually avoid being fired. A moving target is difficult to hit. When you sit tight and wait things out, you increase your vulnerability. Being fired, restructured, downsized, reduced in force, or given a package is now far more common in career patterns. It happens to the best of people—sometimes more than once. These facts do not lessen the trauma. Dealing with involuntary separation is one career strategy that must be faced by more and more professionals as businesses and organizations attempt to adjust to change. There is no doubt that operating from an employed position is the strategy of choice in career transitions, and that to be between assignments greatly increases the degree of difficulty in getting your next job, as well as decreasing your perceived value.

The depth of feeling generated when you find yourself on the outside looking in is far greater than most people anticipate. The human need for security is basic. Unfortunately, the idea that organizations provide security is almost as deep-seated. That concept is one of the root causes of getting caught in cutbacks. You must read situations in advance and take action. Building contributing skills that will transfer easily and allow you to gain a degree of career independence is what needs to be done. Instant independence brings with it the stark reality of having to do all at once the things you should have been doing over an extended period of time.

YOU HAVE
A JOB TO DO

As soon as you get the word that you no longer are needed by your employer, you immediately become self-employed. Your new job is to market yourself. You have just become both marketing manager and senior sales representative of your own business whether you like it or not. You are working full time with a deferred income. Instead of getting paid for your efforts at the end of each two week or monthly period, you will now be paid when you close a sale for your services. Because you can't change the negatives, you might just as well list the positives and get to work selling yourself into your next position.

Plus number one is that you are no longer tied to a dead-end situation. The pressure of being fired is off your back. It's already happened. You don't have to make a gut-wrenching decision to leave. It's been made for you. You are free to work full time at getting involved with a growth opportunity where you can be a part of the action. You can find some place that is on the move and where you are really needed.

If you have ever had to hire someone, you know the relief you feel when you finally find a perfect fit, and he or she comes on board. You now have the chance to be of great help to someone. Your job is to find that someone.

As soon as you get the word that you no longer are needed by your employer, you immediately become self-employed. Your new job is to market yourself.

The pressure of being fired is off your back. It's already happened.

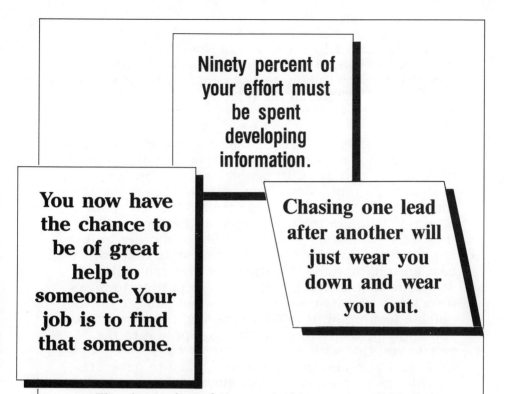

Ninety percent of your effort must be spent developing information.

You now have the chance to be of great help to someone. Your job is to find that someone.

Chasing one lead after another will just wear you down and wear you out.

The dynamics of the workplace are such that at all times and in almost all places there are needs that must be met.

Those in sales will tell you that it is counterproductive to try and sell something until you determine what is needed and who can take positive action.

The way to avoid needless rejection is to seek information and contacts in order to locate potential opportunities. It's definitely a two-step process. Trying to get a job before you qualify and probe leads is the reverse of how the process works. Ninety percent of your effort must be spent developing information. It is only when you come up with a red hot prospect that you will begin selling yourself. You must be very, very professional as you gather data with face-to-face meetings because, of course, even though you are not in a sales mode, you are being evaluated.

You want to make sure you are going after something worthwhile, so investing the up-front time in careful investigation is a smart strategy. Chasing one lead after another will just wear you down and wear you out.

It's far easier to dig out data than it is to apply and interview for jobs. The very process of developing opportunities by talking to key people will put you in the running without all the rejection and negative experiences generated by trying to do step two before step one.

No one sells against the odds. Why should you try it? Spend your time determining what the odds are. Face-to-face contact with people in the know is your objective. You interview them. You want to know where the action is. Is the industry, company, or competitor growing? Who are the key people in that process? If they were you, who would they talk to in order to find out what's happening? Usually the people that have the best information are also the ones who can make decisions to add new people. The temptation to press for a job is almost overwhelming when you are on the outside looking in. It must be resisted because when you apply pressure to yourself, you apply it to the people you talk with. It shows, and it causes negative feelings all around that you can't afford to generate.

Just as preplanned career moves take endless time periods to close, involuntary career transitions often take even longer. Developing large numbers of face-to-face informational meetings is not quick work. You have the advantage of being able to devote your efforts full time to the project, but just as in the preplanned situation, businesses work against their schedules, not

> **The temptation to press for a job is almost overwhelming when you are on the outside looking in. It must be resisted because when you apply pressure to yourself, you apply it to the people you talk with.**

yours. It's great to have an objective of five or six meetings per week, but those who have gone through one of these transitions will tell you that it's not unusual to go two or three weeks with no meeting at all or to have only one meeting per week, in spite of all-out efforts to make contacts and schedule appointments.

This is also the time to put your personal senior advisory network on red alert. Use your schedule flexibility to set up touch-base strategy meetings with as many of your informal advisors as possible. These meetings will generate a few leads for you simply because your friends are focusing on your situation.

> **It is always a good strategy to try and keep yourself out of the pile.**

USING THE CLASSIFIEDS

Although in general classified ads are long shots at best, you will find it difficult to resist the temptation to reply to them during an unplanned career move. Read them for information on which companies are growing where, what is being looked for, and at what approximate price. Pull out only those that seem to be close background fits to give them a try. Ideally, you want to take the ad and see if you can find someone who can give you a referral into the same organization, so that you can go around the employment process. It is always a good strategy to try and keep yourself out of the pile. Failing that, you may have to take a direct shot.

A single-page letter is the bullet to fire. Don't shoot yourself in the foot with a resume (even when they ask for one). Speak only to the elements in the ad. (Don't give salary requirements or history, even if requested.) Pick your strongest point of compatibility and open with it. Don't go into detail. If you worked for an organization that has name recognition, fit that in.

> **A single-page letter is the bullet to fire. Don't shoot yourself in the foot with a resume.**

> **All you are trying to do is to lessen the odds of losing. You are not trying to win.**

> **Take the classifieds for what they are worth. Don't expect major results.**

Your objective is to raise questions, not answer unasked ones. That way you place yourself in the follow-up versus reject pile. Don't be discouraged if after working for hours on a literary masterpiece, you receive either no response or some kind of a form letter. This result is a function of the inadequacies of the process, not of you or the effort you made. The volume generated by ads absolutely overwhelms any attempt for objective or complete evaluation. That is why the brief on-target reply is the method of choice.

In following up ads, you can't predict what will strike a chord. All you know for sure is that evaluating responses is a negative elimination process; therefore, you must do everything you can to avoid being screened out. The less information they have to work on the better. What is enough to raise interest while not enough to cause elimination? That question has no definitive answer. All you are trying to do is to lessen the odds of losing. You are not trying to win. In a negative game that is a reasonable strategy. Blind ads just increase the negative odds. You cannot make this classified ad response effort a primary element in developing new opportunities.

Take the classifieds for what they are worth. Don't expect major results. If you pick up a solid one or two that produces face-to-face meetings, you are ahead of the game. If you don't, you shouldn't feel bad. The numbers are against you.

GETTING THE BEST
FROM OUTPLACEMENT

Part of the process of becoming totally independent against your will is that bad feelings are generated toward those causing your discomfort. Two common strategies are to seek legal counsel and a publisher. You may have grounds for either or both actions. Again, the odds of producing something positive as a result are long.

The general rule of always leaving on good terms is an employer's rule. A wrongful discharge suit may get you an out-of-court settlement that will more than compensate for the effort. Former employers can only give negative references at great personal legal risk. That's their problem, not yours.

One benefit you may be able to extract from your former employer is outside outplacement counseling. This is a service of our friends in the employment

The general rule of always leaving on good terms is an employer's rule.

Former employers can only give negative references at great personal legal risk. That's their problem, not yours.

Outplacement counseling is a service in the employment industry designed to keep them in funds during negative hiring periods.

industry designed to keep them in funds during negative hiring periods. The price is right (for you it's free), so take it. You can go for a better settlement after outplacement, if you find you have grounds. Keep in mind that because the outplacement process is funded by a client company the function provided is a service to the client, not to you. The fees are paid to avoid trouble. Outplacement is an industrial hazardous waste disposal system. It's an adult diaper service. Its purpose is to allow ground zero to cool.

Regardless of the motivation or the underlying purpose, there is value in taking advantage of the process. You will have a base of operation and someone to talk to who can provide some comfort. Keep in mind the "love for sale" nature of your relationship with your outplacement counselors. It's not your money, so take all you can get. Do the things they ask you to do, but of greater importance, do your own thing. Outplacement people spend a great deal of time on introspection, resume construction, and counseling. Do what you have to do in order to have access to whatever support facilities they provide, but keep in mind that the focus of your action must be external not internal. You must be searching for contacts, having meetings, and seeking information directly from potential key people. Time-consuming outplacement exercises are no substitute for the real work of developing information through actual field meetings.

> **Outplacement is an industrial hazardous waste disposal system.**

> **Companies, industries, and organizations don't hire people. People hire people.**

Your so-called campaign cannot be a direct mail marketing effort. It must be a hand-shaking, press-the-flesh endeavor with as many back room meetings as possible. Companies, industries, and organizations don't hire people. People hire people.

People don't hire resumes, backgrounds, or profiles. They hire people they like, who seem to have the potential to fill a need. The more they like you, the more potential they will buy.

Use outplacement services as a base for doing your own thing. Their thing won't do you much harm, unless it takes too much of your time. You should know that it is unlikely to do much more than keep you busy while time passes. Passing time while seeming to do productive things is an underlying if unstated premise of outplacement. All of the things they ask you to do seem to have at least an indirect relationship to making a new career start. Some may actually be of help to you, but the only real help you need is a name, a referral, a lead, another meeting, or a contact that will result in discovering a potential prospect in a growth situation that needs your help.

> **Mental health is just as important as physical health in times of high stress.**

MEETINGS ARE THE ONLY SCORE TO KEEP

Keeping yourself tightly focused on your objective of meeting face-to-face with people will allow you to rank all other activities in accordance with how they support that prime effort. Be polite to your outplacement friends while using them for all that they are worth. This may seem to be a mercenary approach, but they are not exactly angels of mercy themselves, so you are fully justified in treating them accordingly. There is always the outside chance you will run across a person of great value doing outplacement who can be of real help. Accept that gift from on high, but don't expect it.

> **Some of the most positive, dramatic turning points in people's careers are involuntary.**

EMOTIONAL HIGHS AND LOWS

One area of an involuntary career move that is often underestimated is the range of emotional swings that are generated. Separation from close business associates who may be close social contacts as well, the questioning of your personal value to an organization in the face of the ultimate negative evaluation, the long slow steps required to develop a data base of people and opportunities to pursue—all of these contribute to a less than positive view of reality. On the other end is the elation caused by the discovery of great contacts and solid leads in industries or companies that are ideal for your talents. The ups surprisingly are almost more difficult to deal with than the downs. When you get yourself sky high because of a great contact or meeting, be careful. If it doesn't come through—and most don't—you will be riding for a tremendous fall. Typically, during one of these involuntary career transitions, you will come very, very close on several solid situations, and then for no good reason they will come apart. This is very tough to take.

If you need outside professional help to deal with this aspect, by all means get it. It could well be that your medical benefits will fund it, and that is just one more reason to take advantage of what is offered. Mental health is just as important as physical health in times of high stress.

You needn't panic while reading all of this because even though the situation is described realistically, literally thousands of people are moving through these phases every day. Some of your best friends no doubt have been there before you.

They not only survived, but prospered. Some of the most positive, dramatic turning points in people's careers are involuntary. In fact, much of this book is directed toward encouraging you to voluntarily do what many find themselves doing involuntarily. The positive motivation is much more pleasant. The end result, a new career vitality, may be the result either way.

There is no need to make an earth-shaking decision. It's been made. All you have to do is react positively.

You can go in new and exciting directions. You can meet new people and go to new places. You can get a big jump in income. You can get an employment contract or a piece of the action.

You can shift gears to a different size operation. You can sculpture a new lifestyle. You can make a contribution closer in tune with what you have to offer. You need not be underutilized.

In retrospect, all these positive results are possible. Your mission is to get to a retrospective position as efficiently as possible. You must be able to address the negative aspects of an involuntary move positively both for your emotional well-being and for the benefit of future employers. You must acknowledge that you hung in too long; that you didn't read the signals; that you were working for the wrong person. All these positions are understandable when explained with a single sentence or two. No one wants to hear yesterday's weather report. They want to know about the future. What's the forecast? Yesterday it rained. Okay, now it's today; let's see what's in the cards. What's happened is history. What's important is what's happening in the organization you are exploring.

Learning brief comebacks to questions on what caused your move, and being able to shift the focus foreward is a technique you must develop. No one wants the details of "your operation." That's over; what's next is what counts.

You can more than survive an involuntary career move; you can make it a major turning point. If you get a chance at it, recognize it for what it truly is. It's a golden, sometimes once in a lifetime (hopefully) chance, to work full time for yourself to make a first class deal for your efforts. Take all of the positive consequences and use them to deflect and defeat the negatives.

This is not an easy career strategy to follow, but if this is what is dealt to you, there should be no question what to do about it and how best to turn the situation to your advantage.

CHAPTER 11

AGE, GENDER, RACE

> **Power over people is where the most subjectivity in management is° found.**

> **The chain of command system works to the advantage of those running it, not those in it.**

Careers are competitive. Most rules are unwritten. Power over people is where the most subjectivity in management is found. Bias is a fact of life in society in general, in particular industries, in specific companies, and with individual managers. You may not be able to do anything about it no matter how hard you try. The chain of command system taken from the military is almost universally supported. The system isn't fair and it often can't be beaten. It works to the advantage of those running it, not those in it.

DIFFERENCES CAUSE BIAS

The fact that you enjoy what you do, like the place you work, have good relationships up and down in your organization, should not lull you to sleep when it comes to making career progress.

Half of the U.S. workforce is made up of women. Regardless of law, policies, and directives to the contrary, the fact remains that women are an underpaid and often underutilized element taken as a group. If you are in this group, don't deny these facts of organizational life just because you may have reached a personal comfort level.

Understand that those in power think it is in their best interest to keep things the way they are. Managers are paid to avoid risk, to go with the known. Many male managers view women as an unknown (to them) and therefore associate them with risk. It takes a secure male manager to see the fallacy in this strategy.

Being paid for your contributions, recognized for your skill, and promoted to power positions is a legitimate career goal for everyone.

Expecting this to happen out of the goodness of organizational justice is naive. If you are different from those in power in any way, including gender, you must compete more vigorously for what you earn.

One manager was recruited by a large multinational for his professional expertise. Several months after joining the organization, his boss was promoted. His new superior let it be known that few people "brought in from the outside" ever make it with this company.

> **If you are different from those in power in any way, including gender, you must compete more vigorously for what you earn.**

Our manager performed well, made innovative contributions and good progress up the pay scale, until four years later when he was fired. Because he had not paid his dues by coming up through the ranks, by not having been assigned to four or five field locations, by not being a full-fledged member of the inner club, his boss still felt he was holding a position that he had not earned. Sure he had made some mistakes (everyone must in order to get things done) but his errors were, of course, scored unusually heavily against him, and eventually his negative totals were used to grease the rails of departure.

This was a classic no-win situation. Wanting to keep his job, the manager did everything he could, but the judgment had been made at that initial meeting with the new boss. Each performance review was just an evidence-gathering exercise. Our manager's strategy was to wait it out in the hope that his boss would get promoted. He didn't.

If a minor, subjective difference of not being promoted up through the ranks can trigger the negative response of a vice president, can you imagine what real differences can do?

> **Low visibility is essential to career progress.**

KEEP A LOW PROFILE

The fact is that no one can survive the process of being singled out for close, extended scrutiny. Low visibility is essential to career progress. Only when the time is right and under the sponsorship of the power structure can high visibility result in major moves. This process must usually be orchestrated from above. It is called the mentor system, or promotion from within, or the old-boy network. There are exceptions to the process, but the rules will generally apply.

The subjectivity and unfairness of this type of management is the cause of bright, talented people leaving organizations. Unfortunately many people feel that because they are not getting the career rewards they have earned, there is something wrong with them. They must work harder, be more careful, keep better records to justify their actions, take fewer chances—somehow they must play the game better in order to win.

If the unwritten rules are against you, there is no way you can win.

Visibility can be used against anyone who differs in any way.

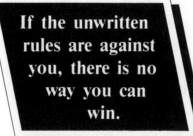

If the unwritten rules are against you, there is no way you can win.

DEAD-ENDED PROMOTIONS

After three years in field assignments, a young black manager was promoted to the home office to gain the background necessary to qualify for future line assignments.

On his first day in his new job, he arrived in his office at seven A.M. At seven-fifteen the division president came to visit. Sort of a welcome aboard gesture. They talked for an hour and a half. It was all over before it had begun. By the time his boss came in at nine, the new manager's career there was over.

The fact is, the president of that division never came down three levels to greet anyone. He made his subjective judgment before the new man had a chance to even begin to fit in. He mentioned to the departmental vice president that he had talked with his new junior from the field and that he was not overly impressed.

Who could have survived the ninety minute inquisition and its resultant final judgment? No one— no one who was black, in that position, in that company. The manager left a year and a half later in spite of every effort his immediate boss made to help him along.

Of course, in some industries and in some companies those who do not fit the mold of those in the power structure have made some career progress. Tokenism comes first; then, sometimes, expanded tokenism follows. Entry-level jobs have opened, an occasional nonconforming manager is brought along and little by little, because of the numbers involved, a

All too often, career moves are channeled to a point where progress appears to be made, but actually these moves are to dead-ended areas out of the mainstream.

Women are promoted to velvet ghetto positions. Once this happens, no matter what a woman's inherent value to the system, she is locked in to no-move disciplines.

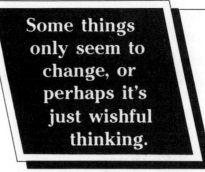

Some things only seem to change, or perhaps it's just wishful thinking.

small degree of latitude is gained outside of stereotypical profiles. People are allowed to make mistakes and not have them recorded indelibly in the book of life. The defensive barriers have been rolled back, but only to the next line. They have not been taken down or put away. All too often, career moves are channeled to a point where progress appears to be made, but actually these moves are to dead-ended areas out of the mainstream.

Women are promoted to velvet ghetto positions. These are assignments that become female-only in actual practice: public relations, human resources, meeting planner, training, management information systems—many have become distinctly pink in flavor. Once this happens, no matter what a woman's inherent value to the system, she is locked in to no-move disciplines.

With minorities, the few available senior assignments are highly public slots in community relations, purchasing, employment—all places where they can be shown off to the outside world to the maximum benefit of the organization.

These practices are not written into the corporate manuals. They are not even designated by top management. They are, however, pervasive in practice. The situation is dynamic, and progress is being made in some areas, but generally things have not changed dramatically. Betty Lehan Harragan's book, *Games Mother Never Taught You*, was published in 1977. Its latest edition has not had a single word changed from the original because the corporate environment it describes still exists. Some things only seem to change, or perhaps it's just wishful thinking.

If these are the facts, what are the strategies that apply against them? What can you do?

> **Who you are, and what you are, and what you can do are under your control. What career results you can achieve are often under the control of others.**

> **It is not in your best interest to be involved in a day-to-day battle or in an extended cold war.**

THE FACTS OF CORPORATE LIFE

First, accept the facts for what they are. They are real. They have nothing to do with you as a person. They affect you only as a member or nonmember of a group. Each career move, each judgment you make must be developed in full light of circumstance. You can neither resent nor deny what you are faced with. You must balance what you find against reason.

If you work for a family-owned organization and you are not a member of the family, that has nothing to do with your value or ability. It has a great deal to do with where you can go in that company. If you are a woman in a male-oriented industry or a minority in a majority-controlled outfit, you have boundaries and barriers to work against or around, but be sure to keep them externalized in spite of all attempts to make you internalize them.

Once you internalize these biases, you lose your personal power to get on with your life. Then "they" really have won and you don't want or need that to happen. Who you are, and what you are, and what you can do are under your control. What career results you can achieve are often under the control of others. It is not in your best interest to be involved in a day-to-day battle or in an extended cold war. It is in your best interest to work in directions that will increase your potential career results. You can come back and attempt to change the system once you have beaten it. You can't change the system in order to beat it.

Do not consider yourself lucky to have the position you do. Do not compare yourself to others in your gender or race. Compare yourself to majority peers or above. Don't segregate yourself out of competitive career paths by looking at how far you have come.

> **You can come back and attempt to change the system once you have beaten it. You can't change the system in order to beat it.**

> **Do not consider yourself lucky to have the position you do.**

> **Do not compare yourself to others in your gender or race. Compare yourself to majority peers or above.**

> **Seek opportunities in mainstream power functions.**

> **Self-promotion through mobility is a good strategy for anyone who is blocked for any reason.**

Think in terms of how far there may be to go and how others are getting there. Seek opportunities in mainstream power functions. Advancements may be offered in high visibility (tokenism) or support functions (dead-ends). It will be difficult to turn those offers down. Always attempt to parlay these types of offers into two-step deals. "If I take this for X months, will I then qualify for a Y power position?"

Evaluate each possible internal move as if you were the only child of the chairman of the board. Is this the job that would be offered to you if that's who you were? If not, then what are the alternatives?

Self-promotion through mobility is a good strategy for anyone who is blocked for any reason. If you see that your opportunities are limited in any way, get your search apparatus into high priority action.

All the rules of normal career movement apply; it's just that you will have to be careful to keep your sights high and your marketability at peak levels.

MEDIOCRITY IS
THEIR STYLE

The system is not set up to develop your potential. It is designed to get a good day's work out of you. Development and advancement are your problem, not the organization's obligation. That's true for everyone, but much more so as a nonmember of the club.

Major corporations can operate effectively with only mediocre talent. Mediocre middle and upper-middle managers often feel threatened by highly visible, highly talented junior professionals.

One woman with seven years in a major communications giant was given a management strike assignment that could not be accomplished with the twelve-hour day-care contract she had for her preschool son. She requested either standby duties or some kind of coverage that would fit with her situation. She was refused and threatened with disciplinary action. She resigned. She was viewed by her manager as being too smart, too bright, and not fitting his image of a dedicated company person. He couldn't see how day-care fit into the equation. Her seven years experience was lost to the company. She, however, still has that experience and is using it for her own future advancement.

The system is not set up to develop your potential. It is designed to get a good day's work out of you.

Development and advancement are your problem, not the organization's obligation.

This kind of managerial myopia can be found in abundance. You can do legal battle whenever it will produce a reasonable return. Your strategic move should always be in your own short- and long-term best interest. You have no obligation to an organization that is not wise enough to protect its investment in you. Fighting against all odds might be the stuff of a best selling autobiography, but even being on the best seller list may not be worth the price.

Instead of the barriers, focus on the routes around, over, or away from the unjust or unjustified obstacles in your path.

If you want to blast on through, that is also your option. If you decide to stand and fight on any issue of bias, be sure you are on strong ground, have as much support as you can get from every source possible and,

You have no obligation to an organization that is not wise enough to protect its investment in you.

Fighting against all odds might be the stuff of a best selling autobiography, but even being on the best seller list may not be worth the price.

last but not least, begin getting Plan B into shape. Your investment in your current position may be too great to walk away from. If that is the case, understand the odds and go for whatever career justice you can get. Give it your best shot internally while at the same time seeking outside counsel.

If you choose to enter the battle and fight for "what's right," pick your spot. You can't just wound your adversary. You need a quick, clean kill. Gradualism doesn't win; it just increases the cost of failure. Independence to go for your objective, whatever it might be, should not be bargained away casually.

> **There is one corporate bias that we are all marching relentlessly toward. Each day we grow a day older.**

> **Market dynamics are what count, not organizational judgments.**

THE AGE FACTOR

There is one corporate bias that we are all marching relentlessly toward. Each day we grow a day older. Our career strategies must be adjusted by age. There is some legal protection in this regard, but our objective is to be smart enough in handling this element so that we will not need the law, with all its complexity and costs, to mix into our alternatives. Sooner or inevitably later, we will all face this bias.

"After thirty-five" covers everyone from there on up. The time span from thirty-five to fifty-five is amazingly fleeting. Falsely perceived security and stability in career matters can cause rude awakenings as age bias creeps in just when many of us feel we have hit our stride. Fortunately, anyone at any age can take charge of where they are going, if they decide to or if they are forced to.

Age strategies dictate that you shift from playing someone else's game to playing your own game by your own rules.

Age requires that instead of covering all the bases, you cover the base that is most likely to bring results.

You must learn to live in the present and continue to develop the future.

The youth culture with its high-energy levels and low-organizational costs is difficult to compete against. The assumed disadvantages of age must be turned around. The vast numbers of contacts, multiple industry exposures, past accomplishments, all should be and can be focused for present and future return. Although organizations may arbitrarily weed you out, you can be assured that if you have a contribution to make, an opportunity perhaps even greater than the one you left can be made to materialize. Market dynamics are what count, not organizational judgments.

Junior readers (thirty-five or thereabouts) should think in terms of preventive strategies that will keep many options open to them as their careers advance. A realistic Plan B is always needed. "This is my objective and this is my backup." Be sure your backup is both desirable and workable.

Age requires that instead of covering all the bases, you cover the base that is most likely to bring results.

Age has been dealt with successfully. You must become a student of the process.

In many corporations where age is used to thin the ranks, you'll be targeted earlier than you ever imagined.

Being who you are is more important than being who you are supposed to be.

It requires that you substitute brains for muscle. Age requires that you take the physical signs of change, acknowledge them, and then identify those areas that have changed positively to provide new strengths.

Age strategies dictate that you shift from playing someone else's game to playing your own game by your own rules. You must accept the fact that you can no longer perform in some arenas. That doesn't mean the end. You just go on to the next phase. You must learn to live in the present and continue to develop the future. The psychological adjustment to age-dictated career shifts are difficult but manageable. Everyone must do it. The sooner you start thinking about these strategies, the better. In many corporations where age is used to thin the ranks, you'll be targeted earlier than you ever imagined.

Complaining about age, fighting it, being beat up by it, aren't the strategies to follow. Age has been dealt with successfully. You must become a student of the process. There are rewarding alternatives. Being who you are is more important than being who you are supposed to be. Age bias is one factor you should be smart enough to recognize and work around.

No matter what your supposed limitations (gender, race, age, lack of an MBA, not a member of the family), there is a strategy that will produce results. Your challenge is to identify that strategy and apply it as best you can. Understanding the external and subjective nature of the bias plus the odds you are up against will equip you to deal with reality. It isn't fair, nor is it easy.

Age bias is one factor you should be smart enough to recognize and work around.

CHAPTER 12

THE OPINIONS OF OTHERS: WHO ARE YOU?

> **The influence of others on your career paths and decisions is greater than you think.**

I t is perhaps the most natural career strategy of all to follow in the footsteps of one's parents. In many parts of the world and for many centuries that was the only career strategy. The influence of others on your career paths and decisions is greater than you think.

To be the first one in a family to attend college is usually the fulfillment of a parent's dream or goal. To settle down (or move out) into a secure job, get married, have a family, stay in the same geographic area—all are parental goals. You may share many or all of them. Either by example or through a general atmosphere of approval or disapproval, you have been exposed to parental standards for better or for worse for all of your life.

Some people want to exceed their parents' accomplishments; some don't want to compete. They want to go in an almost opposite direction. Either way, one is placed in a position of reacting to others.

The influence of others is pervasive in society, and you must take it into consideration as you develop your career strategies. If you have been to a college reunion or two, you will note the exchange of peer approval for career progress. A far more interesting group might be those who do not attend reunions. Many of them have developed different standards and choose not to be compared to their classmates.

LARGER THAN LIFE

We are influenced by the media. We look at the body types of others and feel we must strive to achieve those standards. How one becomes taller or bigger chested is blessedly, for the most part, beyond our technology at present. We seldom stop to think that each person we see on television, even background people in commercials, has survived multiple casting calls and auditions, and has been subjected to the arbitrary tastes of producers and directors, all for the purpose of creating an idealized image.

There are few physically perfect people in real life. Those with idealized careers are just as rare.

Be aware of the power others have over how you see yourself.

> **By mid-career you should have developed sufficient knowledge and experience to want to be your own person.**

The next time you travel, take a closer look at the people in the crowd. Media types are strangely absent. There are few physically perfect people in real life. Those with idealized careers are just as rare.

When people go to the right schools, join the right company, work in the right discipline, make the right moves, live in the right neighborhood, they have elected to adopt someone else's standards as their own.

With all of the influences of others constantly beaming in on you, it is virtually impossible to set clear objective standards for your career strategies. The best you can do is to be aware of the power others have over how you see yourself.

Early in a career it is common to pick a role model and to try and develop the skills and abilities you see in that person. By mid-career you should have developed sufficient knowledge and experience to want to be your own person. You can pick aspects of others that you admire and make efforts to be like them in some ways, but discovering your uniqueness and what you can do with it is much more productive.

You don't have to create your strengths at this point. You already have them. You just have to identify them and then find opportunities to use them. Doing this may distance you from your peers. They may not be comfortable with your progress, but that is not a reason to hold back.

THE PRICE OF
BEING DIFFERENT

A talented staff specialist was fired from a large corporation because of a personality conflict with his boss. Three months later he had not found a new corporate home, but he had picked up a consulting assignment that provided at least temporary income. He attended a three-day meeting of his professional society as a means of staying active in his field with the thought of making possible career contacts. Nothing of substance materialized out of the meeting, but he did notice that the expressions of concern and sympathy were almost overwhelming. "How are things going?" "Is the family all right?" "Hang in there." He was outside of his peer professional's world. They were inside, the only safe and secure place to be.

He never did return to their world. He parlayed his first consulting assignment into his own small business. He did, however, continue to attend his professional society's meetings. Slowly he began to realize that he was an outsider. He had accidentally broken the corporate bonds and established his independence. He had moved away from his peers' career standards. Their continued expressions of concern that he find another corporate position were reflections of the standards they had selected for themselves. Having your own business and being out on your own is generally accepted as being admirable, especially if you can sustain your position. Among this professional group, however, it was subconsciously viewed as a rejection of their values.

> As soon as you decide to up the ante, as soon as you determine you want to go for a higher or different utilization of your talents, you will have to break old ties and seek new ones.

Over the years others in the professional society either made the break by choice or through the choice of others and, rather than returning to another company, stayed out on their own. These "outsiders" began talking to one another at meetings and found that they could be of value in sharing information and providing support during down periods. As early retirements became more common, many of the society members would inquire of the outsiders what it was like out there. In effect, the outsiders' career strategy which had been rejected was slowly becoming more acceptable and even began to become a viable alternative to many.

It is unusual to be able to watch this process evolve. It is far more common to have to part company with your professional peers, if you seek some objective different from theirs. People generally surround themselves with like-minded people. Being different may make you feel vulnerable, but, in fact, it is the group's vulnerability that causes it to close ranks. You will, of course, eventually join another group that shares your new standards.

> **Career strategies that remove you from the "normal" patterns, also remove you from the standards of others.**

> **It's not that you "can't go home again"; it's just that you may not want to.**

When the herd is going in one direction, it is wise to take a long, hard look in the opposite direction.

In a stable society, it is easy to take the course that others do.

As soon as you decide to up the ante, and go for a higher or different utilization of your talents, you will have to break old ties and seek new ones. This is difficult and painful but it is a fact of life. Career strategies that remove you from the "normal" patterns, also remove you from the standards of others.

Parents, by the way, tend to be highly adaptive creatures. They most often will accept their role as spectator or cheerleader in your career adventures, even though you may go in some different directions.

The same is not true for professional peers. You must be prepared to move on, to seek new contacts, to find peers who share your new goals. They are there at every level and at every turn. They are unknown at first, but they surface in time. If you move on to vice president status, you will soon learn to mix with and share perspectives with other vice presidents. If you begin to work in a new industry or new technology, you will find people who will share your new objectives.

So career strategies that stretch your limits carry with them the often unrecognized requirement to break more fully with the standards of the past than is expected. It's not that you "can't go home again"; it's just that you may not want to.

> **It is not necessary to reject the patterns of others in order to set your own standards.**

SOCIETAL MESSAGES AND YOU

Society sends so many messages that some of them get through no matter how much of your own person you profess to be. You don't have to fight against the standards of others, but you should recognize them for what they are and realize that you are not bound by them.

Teenagers go along with whatever is accepted as the norm, no matter how outrageous it may be. In good time they outgrow total reliance on peer values and begin to choose their own directions. It's called finding yourself, and it often takes several years, but it usually happens sooner or later.

In finding yourself at mid-career, you must be sure that the strategies you select fit with both who you determine you are as well as what is going on in the world around you.

In a stable society, it is easy to take the course that others do. In a more fluid environment, the challenge is far greater. When the herd is going in one direction, it is wise to take a long, hard look in the opposite direction.

You need not be a herd creature. You must provide for yourself and whomever else you are responsible for, but aside from that, there are few societal-imposed limits that can't be overcome.

It is not necessary to reject the patterns of others in order to set your own standards. Taking component parts from many other strategies is part of our mosaic building challenge.

By taking a close look at yourself, separate from those around you, you may see more clearly where you do fit with them. Then again, you may see that your goals and needs don't mesh well at all. That's a lesson worth reckoning with at any career point.

REACHING BEYOND

In sports you often hear someone say that a current superstar is his or her idol. To have a hero or someone you admire and attempt to emulate is not bad for starters. What is needed is your own variation of those standards.

One person explained that his career path was following closely along behind one of the leaders in his field. He was comfortable with his progress until someone mentioned that he had so much more to offer than his idol. All of a sudden he was challenged to try and go beyond the pattern he had selected to copy. He couldn't immediately jump to prominence in his profession, but he could begin to think of things that he could do differently than his role model. Expanding your view beyond the standard patterns of others requires the help of anyone and everyone whose opinion you value. It also requires that you listen well, for the worthwhile, stimulating messages are often very subtle.

You may find that breaking out is not for you, or you may find that you have boxed yourself in unnecessarily. No matter what you discover you will benefit by talking yourself through the process. Testing and researching problems, standards, and directions must be a never-ending process.

> **Why let events dictate self-discovery?**

It's amazing that so few people pause to question who they are, where they are going, and why they are going there. Usually this kind of inquiring isn't made unless or until some major career or life event forces a hasty review. Why let events dictate self-discovery? We must expand our views of ourselves if we are to see the strategies that will suit us best. We need not keep to the well-trodden paths before us.

We need not keep to the well-trodden paths before us.

CHAPTER 13

STAGES AND PHASES: SHIFTING VALUES

You should always be a student of what you are doing so the learning challenge never ends.

It is not unusual to have four or five distinct careers.

Whe you first began your career, there was some kind of a phasing in, an initial learning curve. After you understood the standards of performance, both formal and informal, you then set your own norms accordingly and have been working more or less along those lines ever since. At least that's been true for most of us. You should always be a student of what you are doing so the learning challenge never ends.

Many people reject the self-development part of a career strategy and thereby limit themselves. After the initial entry and over-and-above continued professional learning, there is no set pattern to career phases. Most of the models are based on single company linear career paths. Because those are both rare and unrealistic, you should think in terms of shorter and more irregular segments.

It is not unusual to have four or five distinct careers. More and more people are exercising their freedom of choice more and more often. Each time they do this they change phases and values as they go.

THE SWINGING PENDULUM

One woman graduated from nursing school, tried a number of different geographic locations and became a highly valued operating room nurse. When she married, she had the chance to go back to school for a business degree, something she had wanted to do since her school graduation many years before.

Life is not static and her marriage did not last. Once again, as a single person, her economic situation shifted requiring changes in her career strategies and objectives. As her needs changed, sometimes planned and sometimes unplanned, she shifted her values down to twelve-month time periods so that she could work against immediate needs. Once her situation stabilized, she could then extend her horizons somewhat and start to look at thirty-six month blocks.

The idea of working against five-year plans was impractical for her, as it is for most people. She executed all of the basics beautifully. She relied on a network of advisors and professional friends, she explored each move as carefully as she could, and then she pushed herself to make the new piece fit her changing situation.

Few have such a predictable life that they set long-term career goals and then move relentlessly towards them. Too many things happen in the normal course of events that upset carefully made plans. You must learn how to shift your career objectives according to circumstance. Sometimes they will be extended and grand, other times they will be immediate and directed at survival. Fortunately, they will usually shift back again as life's pendulum swings.

> **Few have such a predictable life that they set long-term career goals and then move relentlessly towards them.**

A TRUE STORY

A recent college graduate joined a national consumer products company selling soap to food stores. He had the big company image. He was on his way to what he figured to be an extended career progressing up the ladder to corporate stardom. This progression, by the way, is known as "the big promise."

He enrolled in an MBA night program to build the credentials so valued by his management. However, his immediate supervisor told him to drop night school, because it limited his mobility and would not allow him to make the moves necessary for his upcoming assignments. It seems that both the left and right hand of management had different ideas in even this most revered institution of American business. These were not the only mixed signals, so our now junior professional marketed his initial corporate background to the field sales department of a large instant camera company. Here he found yet another "big promise." He made it through several assignments and geographic moves all the way to a national accounts management position.

By this time he could see that it would take many, many years to make the next two moves to the vice presidential level. He needed a faster-moving organization, if he were to continue to move himself. He tried the fastest thing imaginable when he went to an electronics game outfit on the West Coast. It was a good move because he knew what he was doing in national accounts management, and he made an immediate contribution. The company and industry, unfortunately, turned to mush under his feet. His ability could not influence global events.

Now in his late thirties he had to make his first involuntary move. He had a wife and children and shifted his sights from high speed, high tech to low speed, low tech. Because of his highly visible big company background, he was able to finally reach his V.P. objective in a small footware company specializing in industrial application (work boots with steel toes). He joined a buy-out group with a small piece of the business. Two years later a new president arrived on the scene, and he was given the chance to recover his investment and go elsewhere.

This time he decided to trade "the big promise" for "the small but substantial opportunity." He joined an executive search firm reporting to the president, accepted a V.P.'s title, and went back to selling new accounts one company at a time. He is now just into his forties and has come full circle. He has had five distinct career plans. He is very talented, highly skilled, and now has contacts all through several major industries. He is none the worse for wear. Being able to shift objectives as you move from stage to stage is vital. There are many sunrises and sunsets in each career mosaic.

Before you set yourself up for a mid-life crisis, which often seems to be related to discovering the truth surrounding "the big promise," begin to think about some of the smaller but more attainable victories you can achieve on shorter time frames with more reasonable means. Persistence is overrated in career dynamics.

Being able to shift objectives as you move from stage to stage is vital.

There are many sunrises and sunsets in each career mosaic.

Persistence is overrated in career dynamics.

LONG-TERM GOALS?

"If at first you don't succeed, try again. Then quit. No use being a damn fool about it," or so stated W.C. Fields.

Long-term goals are an interesting concept. Unfortunately, in order to be effective they must translate into some kind of day-to-day activity.

If your basis of day-to-day judgment is tied to objectives set in the distant future, you are not facing the facts of shifting values and situations. You are far better off working in the short term where the degree of certainty is much greater. Each twelve- to thirty-six-month period can have its own set of goals. You may have great flexibility in these time periods, or you may be totally locked in. If you are locked in with zero options for any reason, your goal could well be to figure out a way to increase your breathing space.

You may be well on your way to "the big promise", but don't lose sight of the fact that many others think they are as well. The nature of success in that game is out of the control of the individual. It always comes down from on high.

Career strategies must take into account a broader picture. You must have a social or family life, you must have outside professional and/or civic commitments. You will increase and decrease these elements many times in order to balance them against circumstance. You cannot be rigidly fixed to five-year segments and long-term objectives. Short-term life will not allow it.

You can more easily accept the growth phases of adult life, if you keep in mind that at any time the possibility exists to move in completely unexpected directions, often totally contrary to the stage you are supposed to be in according to some age norm or psychological profile.

Working towards preplanned objectives is so ingrained in our culture that you must be extremely careful not to lock yourself in accidentally while trying to maintain direction in your career management.

One couple had a traditional dual career pattern in action. He was working his way through the underwriting maze in a large insurance company while she was teaching at a private school. They moved back and forth across the country in response to his mobility requirements. In his early forties, he came up against a career block and couldn't get around it. Coincidentally, his wife was approached by a search firm to head an exclusive girls school.

She came in second, but all of a sudden her opportunities opened. She did so well in the search where she lost, she was soon approached again, and this time she was offered a school director's position. Its salary level was above her husband's, and it required a move to the coast. The evaluation committee not only interviewed her spouse too, but agreed to get him a job in their new location. Totally out of character, he shifted all of his goals and objectives to take advantage of his wife's ascendancy.

This situation did not conform to standard long-range plans, objectives, and career norms.

So what? The couple is not miserable because they have a different career strategy. They were smart enough to read reality and shift accordingly. Are they trying to move back with a more conventional arrangement? No way. They have a good thing going and are following it as far as it will take them.

> **You cannot be rigidly fixed to five-year segments and long-term objectives. Short-term life will not allow it.**

SHORT-TERM FLEXIBILITY

Single parents must operate under a completely different set of rules and goals because of the lack of a dual income and the added obligation and expense of children. Conventional wisdom does not apply. Time and space must be created to both produce income and manage family obligations. This amounts to at least two full-time jobs going on simultaneously.

The strain of this situation greatly limits creative or high-risk career strategies. What would normally be standard career transitions become major traumatic decisions. Career holding patterns become an acceptable strategy in order to meet the needs of growing children. Doing it all does not work. Everything has to give. Deciding where career priorities fit and how to adjust is a better strategy than having everything come apart at the seams, perhaps yourself included, while attempting to maintain standard career patterns at all costs. All costs is an excessive price.

Situations change in time and some cannot be forced. When you have flexibility, you can go for it. When you don't, you can't accept the guilt for having to fight it out under less than perfect terms. Your day will come.

There is no such thing as an ideal set of career goals, strategies, time schedules, and moves. You can't be behind if there is no valid norm. Progress, no matter how you define it, is uneven. It's two steps forward and one step back.

What are the reasonable and attainable goals for you in the next twelve to thirty-six months? Set them, but don't be afraid to reset them in the next two weeks if circumstances dictate.

> **There is no such thing as an ideal set of career goals, strategies, time schedules, and moves.**

> **Keep in mind that few careers can be engineered.**

> **What you want or can have now is not what you will want or can have at a later date.**

> **Career dynamics require constant shifts in goals and values.**

Once you accept the concept of short-term flexibility, you will then be open to some positive surprise opportunities. Being open to possibilities is a career strategy that seems idealistic in the face of the realities of life, yet many people have made the break with convention and have discovered a whole new world outside of their perceived career limitations.

Keep in mind that few careers can be engineered. Yes, they must be constructed according to some design, but the elements of that design are not rigid goals and objectives.

What you want or can have now is not what you will want or can have at a later date. The big house on the hill has been the career objective of more than one person, and all too often has proven not to be what was expected.

Career twists and turns defy careful conventional planning. Career dynamics require constant shifts in goals and values. You may not be able to get things to come out your way. The good news is that there may be a better way that you haven't thought about. Don't worry about it. Manage the present dynamic. It will lead to the future.

> **Manage the present dynamic. It will lead to the future.**

CHAPTER 14

SECOND SOURCE INCOME: FINANCIAL STRATEGIES

> **You don't need a get-rich-quick program, but you do need a financial strategy.**

> **Nothing will lock you in tighter to a less than optimum career situation than total financial dependence on your present position.**

Although at this moment you may be struggling with car, rent, insurance payments, and whatever, you have to once again rise above the day-to-day and begin to think about a financial career strategy. Nothing limits you more than a lack of funds. Nothing will lock you in tighter to a less than optimum career situation than total financial dependence on your present position.

Everyone faces the same challenge, and those who rise to it through either standard approaches or through creative tactics reap the benefits of being able to make career choices.

You don't need a get-rich-quick program, but you do need a financial strategy and a means of generating income apart from a primary salary or a single source employer.

DIVERSIFICATION

Your financial goals must be long term, something like a ten-year type plan, rather than a retirement plan. Ideally, your plan should not rely totally on investment income. Once you are certain you are working from a sound fundamental base, you should attempt to be creative if possible.

Add up total current debt and begin to make a serious attempt to reduce it. Getting this part of your house in order is important. Next, go back to basics and set up a reasonable savings program. Avoid giving every conceivable expense priority over your savings. It takes discipline to build savings. You are not just trying to build a nest egg. You are trying to organize yourself in order to act on career options if and when they materialize. You are building financial room to breathe and move. This is an important savings goal which is worth more than any major purchase you may presently be focusing on.

One expense that is often taken as a given is insurance. It is important to shop your insurance costs annually. Don't get emotionally attached to policies or agents. Insurance companies are constantly developing new products to be competitive in the marketplace.

> **You are not just trying to build a nest egg. You are trying to organize yourself in order to act on career options if and when they materialize.**

You don't have to become an expert in the field, but you should talk to one every now and then so that each policy or contract you are paying on is fully justified.

Building home equity is more important than figuring out how best to use it. Get it first. Once it is part of your plan, you can then determine where it will fit in. It may be a base for future educational expenses or it may allow for the buy-in to a small business. The tactics of what to do with your home equity can't be a consideration unless and until you have it to work from.

As your career progresses, you can do all kinds of things to increase independence through diversification.

One manager for a farm machinery company also owned several hundred acres of his family farm. He rented the land on a share crop basis and managed its productivity part time on weekends. By carefully selecting products, he built a solid supplemental business that was run by someone else. He took some of the income (never enough for him to live on full time) and invested it back in the farm. He used a small portion to finance the buying of some inner city rental property which further diversified his income sources. In his late fifties he was phased out of his job, but his outward bound package included his medical and retirement benefits. He then went to work for an association as an internal consultant for a respectable salary. All the pieces add up nicely now that he is in his sixties. He is well diversified. He is not independently wealthy, but he has built himself some financial living space.

You don't have to turn your life over to a professional financial planner, but it doesn't hurt to talk with two or three of them.

THIRD PARTY PERSPECTIVES

You don't have to turn your life over to a professional financial planner, but it doesn't hurt to talk with two or three of them and let them give you an assessment of your situation, along with some ideas on strategies that might work for you.

There is no obligation to buy anything from these professionals. They recognize that they sell services that you may or may not use.

Their third party perspective, however, can uncover some red flags or areas of opportunity that you may not be aware of at first glance. Working with a financial planner is the same as dealing with a doctor, lawyer, or pharmacist. You want someone with credentials, that is respected in the community, that you trust, and hopefully who has a somewhat conservative philosophy. Selecting who to work with or even whether to go with an outside expert is a matter of personal judgment. Keep in mind that the advice given by these experts will always have a bias towards products which provide them income.

OUTSIDE INCOME

A manager for a company that sells high school rings and yearbooks was asked to do a commencement talk for one of his client schools. He checked back with his boss to be sure everyone was in sync and accepted the engagement which produced a small honorarium. Over a few years word got around that this man had a good message, well delivered for that type of audience. He now does ten or twenty commencement speeches each graduation season. His speaking talents bring in other bookings throughout the year which in no way interfere with his full-time job. He has developed an independent second source income. He plans on increasing his bookings as the years go on and eventually phasing into platform speaking as his next career.

Another corporate professional took his guitar-playing talent and began to work wedding receptions on weekends with his brother who played bass. Little by little he accumulated all of the electronic and lighting equipment necessary to do company party dates. He now has a four-piece show band with feature singers and a network of on-call players to cover almost any occasion. None of this activity interferes with his full-time job. All of his bookings come by word of mouth and find their way into his home answering machine. His Decembers are hectic months each year. He is good at what he does. He has further diversified by taking some of his profits and using them to fund the financing of a rental property or two.

TWO ARE BETTER THAN ONE

An obvious source of secondary income is, of course, the dual income generated by two career couples. By living on one or one-and-a-half incomes, you can generate investment capital. Step two means getting it into areas that will provide additional income, or at least appreciation or growth.

The challenge is to distance yourself from total dependence on one income source.

A complete secondary income source doesn't just appear overnight. You may try several ideas before you hit on something that will produce revenue. You may start small and have it build over time.

The challenge is to distance yourself from total dependence on one income source.

The idea is to seek opportunities by always being on the lookout for a chance to generate cash.

One-third of the college faculty in the U.S. are part-time teachers. Many do not have advanced degrees but merely work as instructors or lecturers in their area of career expertise. Teaching one night a week will not make you financially independent, but it will generate income apart from your primary job.

> **Deferred income plans are not designed to provide independence, but dependence by holding people in place over extended periods of time.**

> What must be done, must be done, but don't lose sight of the things that should be done.

KEEP SOME OPTIONS OPEN

Company savings programs and stock purchase systems are better than nothing, but the vesting period may leave you considerably short of real capital appreciation if you must leave for any reason. Keep in mind that these deferred income systems are not designed to provide independence but dependence by holding people in place over extended periods of time.

If you are in the process of bringing up a family, your opportunities to build any kind of financial independence may be completely overshadowed by

> **Make the effort to uncover any income source that can be maintained apart from current employment.**

> **You can't produce career financial security without some kind of diverisity.**

your efforts just to stay even. You may have to put career strategies on hold for a few years in order to cover heavy expenses. What must be done, must be done, but don't lose sight of the things that should be done. Scale back your efforts at independence if you must, but try not to completely shut them down.

You can't produce career financial security without some kind of diversity. The risk of going with one source is too great.

Current lifestyle and future costs of education for children may seem to rule out everything in the way of supplemental income plans. Don't let them. Make the effort to do everything you can to uncover any income source that can be maintained apart from current employment. Equity in property may be the only appreciation you can afford. That is better than nothing and, in many cases, better than many other programs.

> **Secondary income sources are like emergency rations in times of need.**

> **Second source income is one of the most difficult career strategies to master.**

> **It is said that the best way to get rich quick is to do it slowly.**

You can't expect everything to just work out, if you don't put in the planning effort as you go along.

Do a review now and get a couple of outsiders to go through the numbers with you.

It is not unusual to discover that you are better off than you think.

Secondary income sources should not be evaluated in terms of whether or not you could live on them. They are like emergency rations in times of need. They will extend your time limits during a transition. They will give you some flexibility in deciding on career strategies and moves. They sometimes have the potential of being scaled up in some way to make a major contribution.

The strategy of developing additional income sources is a necessary part of life, if you are going to be able to weather the occasional career storms which are just about inevitable.

Begin with standard savings and investments and then be on the lookout for whatever will be workable for you. Get something going early in at least a small way. Second source income is one of the most difficult career strategies to master. Don't dismiss it out of hand as being impossible. If you keep working at it, you will make some progress. Time is on your side. Use it. Don't let it just pass on by. It is said that the best way to get rich quick is to do it slowly.

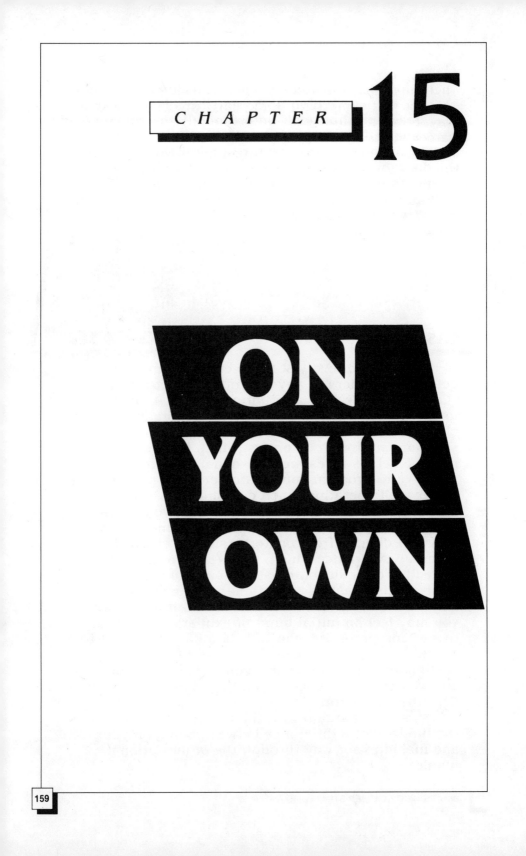

CHAPTER 15

ON YOUR OWN

If independence is a valid career objective, and it is, then having your own business is one way of reaching that goal. Unfortunately the courses and books on entrepreneurship bear little relation to reality. Business plans, venture capital, your name on the door (or at least the stationery), all have neat little segments in the mythology of going out on your own. They are similar in approach to the books on making love. They fail to tell you how to find the perfect someone to make love with.

> **"Cash in" is the only accounting term you must understand.**

CASH IN

The focus of every start-up endeavor must be on getting customers to pay for your product or service. "Cash in" is the only accounting term you must understand. Once you get cash coming in, everything else is manageable. Cash buys time. The more cash you can generate from customers (which is renewable revenue versus investment revenue), the more time you will have to broaden your customer base, product lines and overall operation. Each customer is a source of income. Unlike working for a paycheck, you must adjust to working for a fragmented income supply provided directly from customers. It's a completely different experience which, while easy to write about, is incredibly difficult to adjust to in actual fact.

Spending cash is easy. Generating cash is the single element in business that makes it go. So while you may feel an initial burst of exhilaration in being free of corporate life, you will soon have to adjust to a new kind of dependence—the reliance on your customers to provide your income. When they do, it is an awesome experience. When they don't, it can only be described as terror.

This little bargain with the entrepreneurial devil is the fundamental difference between being on your own and making your way through the organizational jungle.

IF YOU SUCCEED,
YOU DID IT RIGHT

Thousands of people accept this new way of business life every year. Some are forced into it because they have no other alternatives. Some are pushed into it out of sheer frustration with their current situation. Some make calculated moves into it with detailed plans and schedules. Any way you approach it, it can be made to work.

Because business at any level is far more art than science, you can do almost everything right and by the book, yet still fail. You can also do almost everything wrong and luck out and succeed. Factors that are beyond your control are often the governing factors that spell success or failure. The knowledge that even though you are independent things are still out of your control produces the underlying insecurity inherent in the process.

If all this is true, why would any sane individual want to go out on the thin edge and risk falling off? The answer is that the love of the up side, the possibility of winning, the chance to sustain one's self through one's own efforts by personal rules subject only to the marketplace are so powerful that it clouds the mind (as it must). The real odds are not carefully evaluated nor accepted. There are always thousands more reasons why not than why.

You will soon have to adjust to a new kind of dependence—the reliance on your customers to provide your income.

Because business at any level is far more art than science, you can do almost everything right and by the book, yet still fail.

There are always thousands more reasons why not than why.

Emotional decisions, when they turn out favorably, are just as good as cold calculations.

Emotional decisions, when they turn out favorably, are just as good as cold calculations. This is a fact of life that is difficult to adjust to, but it is more or less a real part of being on your own.

Not every venture ends up in the Fortune 500. Those that do cannot be used as examples. What is far more valid, if you are contemplating an entrepreneurial move, is the model that goes from start-up to moderate stability over a period of five to ten years.

Easing into the entrepreneurial water is not as drastic as jumping off the organizational bridge.

You don't want learning experiences. You want to know what you are doing.

DON'T JUMP OFF THE ORGANIZATIONAL BRIDGE

One of the best ways of going out on your own is not to go completely out on your own. Stay where you are. Do a full day's work for your organization. Begin working nights and weekends for yourself. See if you can generate income part time. An ideal situation is to be dragged out on your own almost against your will by those wanting your new product or service. Easing into the entrepreneurial water is not as drastic as jumping off the organizational bridge.

The one thing you don't want to do is make silly mistakes. You don't want learning experiences. You want to know what you are doing. Studying a venture and doing it are two different things. The more hands-on, directly related experience you have, the better. Changing career fields and starting a new business at the same time multiply risk by exponential amounts. You want to know as much about what you are doing as possible so that there are no surprises. Clean breaks from one field and start-ups in new areas can be made, but that type of strategy is what contributes to the high failure statistics. Ease in. You can be innovative, daring, and creative after you have become established.

WHAT ARE YOU GOING TO DO?

Finding an area where there is little or no competition can mean one of two things. You have either discovered a new untapped market or you may be going into a business that hasn't worked or won't be profitable, and that's the real reason no one else is doing it. New ideas combined with start-up situations often reduce the amount of time you will have to get off the ground. Even though it's not very glamorous to be doing something someone else has already done, it might be very smart.

A national accounts manager in data communications watched his organization bring in a new crop of MBA's. He saw the handwriting on the wall.

Reorganization was coming. He had been through this same process in four other companies. The time was right to go for it on his own. The question was what to go for.

Each holiday season as a hobby, he made bird houses as presents. He liked to make them and he was good at it. He figured that they could sell for about seven dollars each. With some rough calculations, he estimated that if he automated his home workshop as much as possible, he could turn out about one bird house per hour.

Although it would have made great cocktail party conversation to be able to say he was in the bird house business, he wisely chose not to make that move.

Because he lived in a rapidly growing town and was well known from serving on its many boards and commissions, he decided to explore a service business. He had done extensive travel in his many assignments and had used many of the local travel agencies. A quick survey indicated that the nearest competition was in the next town, and that because of a change in ownership, the market might be right. Four franchise operations all had about the same fees and didn't seem to offer much in the way of personal attention and assistance. He was able to hire two professionals who had worked in the industry for several years, and by investing his capital in his own computer system and airline software rather than in franchise fees, he was able to get himself established.

Bird houses were where his heart could have been. Going into a stock business was not as glamorous. He wisely did the one and kept the other as a hobby. He relied upon his general business skills and hired in the specialized knowledge he needed to begin.

His market looks strong. All the pieces are in place. He has a good location, good people, and good contacts. If all goes well, he should have a good business. It's that simple and that difficult all at the same time.

The sooner you get down to the basics the better.

You have to adjust to working without a net.

UNDERSTANDING HOW TO SELL

There are few businesses that have succeeded without some measure of selling skills. Someone has to convince someone else that it is in the mutual best interest of both parties to do business together. That's what brings in cash.

Those same skills are needed to attract talent, funding, credit, and of course bigger and bigger or more and more customers. If you are not comfortable selling ideas, products, or services, be careful, because face-to-face sales contact is a key element in almost every start-up business.

Businesses that require up-front investments or long start-up times or new technology are all governed by the same rules eventually. The sooner you get down to the basics the better. Keep overhead and investment to a minimum. Get some way of generating cash from customers at the earliest possible date.

You don't have to be a genius. You have to be able to provide something of value and have enough people pay for it to allow you to build a business. You have to adjust to working without a net. You have to take the successes, as minor as they may be, and blow them all out of proportion so that these victories will emotionally carry you through the disappointments that come with the overall experience.

Confidence and courage in the face of negative reality are again easy to write about, but if you can't generate them within yourself, you won't last very long. Managing success is easy. Managing failure in small doses is a bear.

> **Managing success is easy. Managing failure in small doses is a bear.**

> **Partnerships of all kinds are difficult to make work under the best of circumstances.**

PARTNERSHIPS

There is a general feeling that there is security in numbers and that a partner or two will share the burden, making a start-up more manageable.

Partnerships of all kinds are difficult to make work under the best of circumstances. A general rule in entering into one is always to set the terms of dissolution. That being said, if you can find someone whose skills are completely different from yours and very necessary, someone who you are willing to risk your life on, you may have a piece of the puzzle that will make a new venture work.

Keep in mind that adversity is the rule. It is bad enough bringing it upon yourself and trying to work your own way out of it without having someone else adding to the magnitude of the process or problem.

As with any career strategy, be it a straight company-to-company move or a major career shift, things take far longer than the best plans indicate.

Going off on your own is no exception. Every step has an extended time factor. Expenses run higher and income takes longer to generate no matter how conservative your estimates.

If you want to get yourself into your own thing, you have to begin exploring and making contacts as far in advance as possible. Reaching for opportunities on a continuing basis will eventually produce them. The more possibilities you can generate, the better will become your judgment on what might work for you.

You can read the business opportunities section of the business press, but keep in mind that these are mostly people selling their services to you. These are their businesses. There are real opportunities out there but, as with anything else, they require digging. The more you look, the more you see. Look for the element that gets customers to give you cash. That is always the central concern.

If you read the stories of how others have done it, be careful of the editorial license used in the writing. Things are not always as described in the literature. Try and come up with what made the operation go. Unfortunately, timing and good luck or circumstances that were not planned on are major elements in success stories and therefore can't be duplicated. Few books or articles are written on those ventures that don't make it. They, of course, are in the majority and often are more instructive than the successes.

Reaching for opportunities on a continuing basis will eventually produce them.

The only thing that is like your own business *is* your own business. It's a feeling and experience unlike any other.

GO MEET SOME PEOPLE WHO ARE DOING IT

Local small business associations meet regularly, and while their programs might not be of much value, those attending them are a gold mine of real life adventure stories which should be tapped. You will not only get some of the facts of start-up business life but, almost as important, the feelings as well.

It is hard to believe how getting paid every six months on an indeterminate schedule will affect your life. Ask people how they managed.

Negotiating for yourself on critical contracts or relationships, when the results are life and death matters for your business, is an area for which corporate life does not prepare you. Talk to those who have done it and ask them to share some of their stories. This kind of research is invaluable.

Straight commission capital equipment sales is one of the few careers that comes anywhere near the ups and downs of dealing on a day-to-day basis for your existence. Even then you have some kind of corporate backing during start-up and eventually some flow of business during order cycle swings.

The only thing that is like your own business *is* your own business. It's a feeling and experience unlike any other.

The problem you must face in negotiating is the lack of power you bring to the table. The golden rule of business applies. Those who have the gold make the rules. You have to be a strong person to get favorable terms or, in some cases, any terms at all. Dealing for your business life is a unique challenge that is difficult or impossible to prepare yourself for.

With all of this being said, going on your own can be the best of all worlds. You don't even have to be successful in order for it to be a great life. Just being out there, in the hunt and doing well enough to stay there is a reward worth the risk.

The longer you stay in the hunt, the more likely you are to make a hit or two.

> **The golden rule of business applies. Those who have the gold make the rules.**

> **If it were easy, everyone would be out there. It's not and they aren't.**

> **The longer you are able to stay out on your own, the smarter you will become at extending your effort.**

The longer you are able to stay out on your own, the smarter you will become at extending your effort.

Extending yourself and not being restricted by someone else's judgment as to what you can or cannot handle has a satisfaction all its own. Finding out what you are made of is an enlightening experience. You can almost be assured it is far more than your best estimate.

Economics will always play a part. Your obligations will hold you right where you are unless through dual income or a part-time start-up you are able to get some cash flow going. If it were easy, everyone would be out there. It's not and they aren't.

Look carefully into the strategy of going on your own. The rules are different than commonly believed. They are manageable. It can be done. The sooner you get started on your own, the more time you will have to make it work for you, or the more chances you will have to try again, if it doesn't go on the first try or two. Don't make it a forlorn wish. Make it a real career option by beginning the up-front exploration now. It doesn't cost you anything to look and read and meet people who have been there.

Once you become familiar with what it's really like out there, it becomes easier to project yourself into that kind of a free-form world.

It may not be for you. Or it may not be for you now, but don't rule this strategy out by not taking a long, hard look at what it's all about. Sooner or later you might decide it is for you. The fact that few people turn back from this career strategy unless forced back by circumstances should indicate to you that something worthwhile is out there. It is!

CHAPTER 16

RETIREMENT: A CAREER GOAL?

> **I can think of few more damaging quantitative ideas than the age sixty-five retirement milestone.**

> **To want to stop at sixty-five is to want to stop a basic drive of life. It can be done, but at great cost.**

Retirement at age sixty-five is an idea that was developed over a hundred years ago in Germany in order to set up the bureaucratic procedures in Bismarck's social security system. The number, as far as we know, was an arbitrary figure somewhere near male life expectancy at the time.

I can think of few more damaging quantitative ideas than the age sixty-five (or thereabouts) retirement milestone.

The age sixty-five arbitrary deadline has cut short many highly productive careers, and even lives. It has inflicted reduced living standards on people who deserve much more. It has caused involuntary geographic relocations that have separated family and friends by thousands of miles.

In business, it has done grave things to retard growth, prevent risk at the expense of gain, and discourage innovative thinking in general.

> **The gold watch myth is a path that uses and discards people.**

> **If retirement is a driving force in your career strategy, be sure it's actually worth the effort.**

A FALLACY IN YOUR FUTURE

Before you set retirement as a career goal and develop your strategies to get there, you had best begin to meet retired people and see what it is you are trying to achieve.

There is one definition of life that states that if something moves, it's alive. If it doesn't, it's dead. Cutting back, reducing motion, reducing activity, reduce life. Shifting careers to compensate for a changing lifestyle is a reasonable strategy at any age, but calling an abrupt halt to what you are doing and then attempting to go on a perpetual vacation seldom works well.

We are goal-driven beings. We set out things to do great and small and then work towards them. We earn a living, we may do well. We start families, we help them grow. We build careers or organizations, we bring others along. We use our talents to make a difference, to make a mark. We want to contribute.

To want to stop all that at sixty-five is to want to stop a basic drive of life. It can be done, but at great cost.

The gold watch myth of joining an organization in your youth and then proceeding to give decades of service in return for an engraved watch at retirement has a number of flaws. First of all, both you and the organization must be around and be somehow compatible for an extended number of years. Secondly, the symbolic gold watch says that it's over. The number of people that follow this path are blessedly few. It is a path that uses and discards people.

One company designed a corollary to the gold watch by giving all employees a Mickey Mouse watch on the first day of work. They were told that each time they looked at that watch they should ask themselves if they were having a good time, if they were happy in what they were doing; if not they should do something about it.

Long-term payoffs are risky career goals. If retirement is a driving force in you career strategy, be sure it's actually worth the effort.

> **There is no reason why you must make an abrupt career shift at an arbitrary age.**

> **You don't want pre-retirement planning. You want a valued new position in a field you select.**

SMOOTH SHIFTS VERSUS ABRUPT CHANGES

Think about developing some career strategies that will allow you to avoid Bismarck's curse. There is no reason why you must make an abrupt career shift at an arbitrary age. Early retirement is organizational house cleaning. Economically it may be an offer you can't refuse, but it still represents an abrupt change.

Smooth career transitions are in your best interest at all stages. You are far better off testing relationships, skills, markets, locations, lifestyles a little bit at a time rather than all at once. You don't want pre-retirement planning. You want a valued new position in a field that you select. You may want to just shift responsibilities where you are and keep on doing what you do best. You may have to own the place to do that, but perhaps not. There are some enlightened corporations that recognize value at any age. Evaluate that possibility now, not at age sixty. This is one career strategy you have to be well out in front of.

> **Testing alternatives years in advance under zero pressure is the strategy to develop.**

> **Instead of looking for a single alternative, broaden your view by thinking about numbers of alternatives.**

DEVELOP A FUTURE ON THE OUTSIDE

Building a consulting practice over a number of years is a strategy followed by many in order to stay in the ring. The in-and-out nature of consulting may not be for you, but the time to find out is well in advance of making it a career choice. Do some free consulting for civic or volunteer organizations, or try a small paid client or two in order to get the feel for the process. Testing alternatives years in advance under zero pressure is the strategy to develop.

Small business may be an interest, but it is better to begin it as a hobby or as a weekend or sometime thing so that you can first decide if it has merit, and second, determine how best to scale it up to whatever size you judge to be appropriate. One benefit in all this early exploration is that you may find something far ahead of potential retirement age and just decide to go do it. Discovering opportunities is a part of the career mosaic process from the very beginning and will often take you down an unanticipated path. It is difficult to be a winner if you are not out trying new things, trying to explore options, trying to find something you may not even be looking for.

There is a belief that a wise career strategy will direct you to look for a move, an opportunity, a single, focused task. One surprise that many have discovered is that doing a number of different things, sometimes not tightly related, will add up to almost a full-time occupation. Part-time or seasonal opportunities have a way of developing complementary elements that fit together. Instead of looking for a single alternative, broaden your view by thinking about numbers of alternatives.

The time is always right to explore this potentially exciting mix of interests and strengths but especially in a pre-retirement exploration. If you find one good but small piece of the puzzle, don't discard it but see what other pieces may fit.

What you want to do may not be enough of a challenge or may not support your economic lifestyle, but it may be able to be done in small blocks of time. That's an indication that you are on the right track. Get that one piece up and running while continuing to see what other elements would fit your needs. Multiple answers to later career moves can be the best answers because of the flexibility of the mix and match nature of the process. Part-time means a partial commitment. It means that you then have part-time for whatever else you may wish to do.

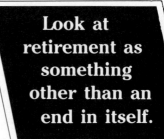

Look at retirement as something other than an end in itself.

TRANSITIONAL CAREERS

Mid-career may seem like an inappropriate time to give much thought to retirement, but whether you plan on a formal retirement or plan to lead up to these many alternatives will influence what you are doing right now.

The totally planned approach is self-defeating. Too many things can happen along the way that will upset blueprint career planning. The one thing that you can bet on or hope for is that age is predictable. Trying to make it productive and worthwhile is the same objective you are working on at present.

Focusing forward and developing options is the identical strategy we have been employing in each career phase discussed so far, and retirement is no different. Look at retirement as something other than an end in itself. The career objective is freedom to explore many options. Management of lead time always increases options. The technique of projecting to what you hope to be the end result and taking a realistic rather than glamorized look at just what it is you are trying to accomplish will put things in a clearer perspective.

CLASSIC RETIREMENT

Consider shifting smoothly into a transitional career. After all, a departing family frees up home equity to invest in a new business development. The maturing of children opens up career options so you can now help them with their business ventures. Reduced family expenses allow a different group of career opportunities to be considered by formerly senior level executives. No longer being responsible for international or geographically dispersed operations allows for reduced travel and concentration on local matters for perhaps the first time. How refreshing it can be to apply your business expertise to local school and government matters.

When you make a major career shift because of age, it is wise to try to keep as many of the touchstones of your background as you can. One district sales manager at age 52 had his district office eliminated (and his job along with it). He stayed right in the same field and right in the same area with all the same customers he had been dealing with for years. What he did was to identify a competitor that dealt through manufacturers' representatives. He contacted the head of the local outfit that had the line, and signed on as a salesman. His income took a dip because of the commission structure and long selling cycles involved with capital equipment, but he didn't have to learn the business, products, or territory. He had to make the mental adjustment from the management of a group of sales people to the management of his own sales territory, but the adjustments were surprisingly minor. And he felt good about working in an area he knew well. He managed to go through one of life's major transitions with minimal upheaval. The whole process took about six months. It wasn't easy, but he did it.

Another senior manager shifted from doing to teaching. He had the time and income reserve necessary to go back to school for a master's degree. He then obtained a part-time college assignment which he later converted to a full academic load. He just retired for the second time in his late seventies. The same move can often be made without getting academic credentials. If sold in properly, your background can be the deciding factor.

More and more people are making major contributions at more and more advanced ages. It is becoming more and more acceptable. Begin to take a look at this group and see what they are doing, because sure enough, this is a group you will be joining. They are setting some standards that are hard to believe. Explore the final phases of your career strategy just as aggressively as you plan all other moves. See what others have done; go talk to them. Look at your strengths and desires. Try and set up your finances in reasonable order to allow for maneuvering space. Figure out how you can best contribute and what you can expect in the future. Taking all these apparent lemons and turning them into lemonade is the challenge of dealing with a career system that emphasizes youth over experience.

> **Begin to take a look at this group and see what they are doing, because sure enough, this is a group you will be joining.**

> **Explore the final phases of your career strategy just as aggressively as you plan all other moves.**

> **More and more people are shifting careers as an alternative to formal retirement.**

> **You must learn to produce results while providing for your career safety at the same time.**

HERE'S TO YOUR HEALTH

In talking with and visiting retired people, one thing that concerns them most is health. It's not necessary to become a health nut in your thirties in order to assure a long healthy life, but a reasonable strategy of healthful practices becomes a vital part of an extended career strategy.

One complements the other in some strange ways. When you have important things to do, you generate extended periods of good health.

Doctors will tell you that the recovery period for self-employed persons is as much as ten times faster than their organizational counterparts, because of their drive to get things done.

The link between work, having things to get done, having a mission, and having the health needed to accomplish what you want is not scientifically proven. Circumstantially the evidence is substantial. You don't have to prove it. All you have to do is take it in as a factor in career strategy. Work is a fact and factor in life. Play is also important, but has never proven itself to be worthwhile on a full-time basis at any career stage, and certainly not as you get older. Play now. Do as much as you can. Extend yourself. Take the vacations. Go for the sabbatical. Lengthen the trip by a few days. Take someone along. Don't hurry play time. Don't postpone it. It is far better taken in bits and pieces as you go along rather than setting up your life for full-time play at the far end.

Deciding never to retire is now a real option. Just add a few more chips to the mosaic. More and more people are shifting careers as an alternative to formal retirement. You might as well begin thinking in these directions, because if the trends continue, this could be the rule by the time you get there.

One thing that you must accept now is that your career life does not end at age sixty-five.

What it will be is a challenge that you should begin seriously considering. It could have some real consequences on strategies you are working on right now. It's always a good idea to select an ideal outcome and then work it backwards to the present. This kind of pre-retirement planning is far more productive than the typical calculations of scaled-back income and how to adjust to a reduced lifestyle—which, of course, is actually a reduced life.

CHAPTER 17

PUTTING THE STRATEGIES TOGETHER

> **You must learn to produce results while providing for your career safety at the same time.**

> **Misplaced organizational loyalty will not be rewarded. It is a poor investment.**

The corporate ship is no longer reliable transportation across the career ocean. Small craft sailing, navigation, and even swimming are skills that everyone must master for survival, as well as arrival at worthwhile career destinations.

When you go up into the rigging, all jobs must be able to be done with one hand so you can hold on with the other. One hand for yourself, one hand for the ship was the rule in the days of sail. It was in everyone's best interest that you not fall from a mast or yardarm.

That rule has new and deeper meaning in today's career strategies. You cannot give one hundred percent to your job, to your company, and to the tasks you are assigned. You must learn to produce results while providing for your career safety at the same time. Loyalty must be divided with first consideration going to your goals, your family, and your life progress. You do not owe an organization loyalty beyond the requirements of integrity and honesty. Misplaced organizational loyalty will not be rewarded. It is a poor investment.

There are isolated examples of organizations taking care of their own, but those are rare exceptions and should not be a basis of your career strategy. The relationship you have with an organization is always one of a buyer and seller of services. It may be long and fruitful or short and sweet. Either way, you are a vendor, not a member of the family.

As you live the chapters of your biography and assemble the pieces of your career mosaic, you will have the chance to go in many different directions. At some stage you will opt to play it safe. You may have to. At other points you may choose to make some moves, to see what the future holds, to stretch yourself, and find out what you are made of. There are no clear cut rules. Lean on your trusted advisors. Take your time; speed is grossly overrated. If you miss an opportunity because of your unwillingness to make a quick move, write it off as not for you. Things have a way of coming around.

> **Make your own strategic definition of success.**

SETTING YOUR SIGHTS

It's important that you develop an overview of what you are doing with your life and career. The tactics of the next move often fill the horizon. It is human nature to allow a vice president's chair or some other immediate objective to just about block out the sun. Intellectually, you can reason to a set of values that will put things in perspective, but when faced with the actuality of the big chance, of the big challenge, of the big price to pay, it is far more difficult to expand to the big picture. Do it now with a clear head and clear vision.

Make your own strategic definition of success. There is far more to it than the big job and the big money. You may extend your reach as opportunities develop, but having your feet on the ground and all elements in balance is the stance that will allow you to go with your strengths and do the things that are most meaningful.

Most of us will not make it to the ranks of the superrich or superfamous. Count your blessings because few who hit those plateaus handle them well. You may think, "I would do it differently; just give me the chance." All of those who are there thought the same thoughts. If you do, for some reason, happen to arrive in those ranks (and it is difficult to think of anyone who made it there without one, wanting to be there and, two, paying all of the prices that go along with it), you will have your shot at trying to balance the heavy load that comes with the position. Best of luck to you.

It is more likely that you will hit a level of achievement somewhat short of regular appearances on the nightly news. Adjust your career scoring system to more closely reflect those values that are meaningful to you. That doesn't mean lowering your sights or settling for less than you are worth, but it does mean evaluating what you do best, what you can contribute, what effect you will have on others, and what of lasting value you may leave behind when your time in the ring winds down.

> **The rewards of family will almost always exceed the rewards of career.**

LOOKING CLOSE TO HOME

An often discounted career strategy is the building of a family. Children are not a minor consideration, nor are they just the concern of women. In retrospect, bringing up a family has been the major life task of millions of people. Passing on a value system, providing support, providing education are all substantial undertakings and are not add-ons to a career strategy. They are the focus of many career strategies and should be considered as such.

Doing a good job of parenting can produce incredible returns. Fitting that piece of the mosaic into the picture seldom gets the recognition or priority it deserves. Your life needn't revolve around your children, but striking a balance between career and family is part of the challenge of strategy development.

The rewards of family will almost always exceed the rewards of career, so if you are fortunate enough to have the opportunity to bring up a family, you may have found a large portion of your life's work. The fact that every person of value has had two other people responsible for him or her from a previous generation is seldom reflected on. That effort is not often thought of in considering life goals and career strategies.

Instead of making the big splash with our lives, it could well be that the small substantial ripples, the way we affect others in many, many ways, will be our contributions.

SO WHAT IS A CAREER STRATEGY?

One of the insights that we gain after only a few years into our careers is that things are not exactly as they appear. There are many intermediary moves that are totally unexpected. Change is a constant. A career strategy that is open to change is more likely to work long term than one with fixed, far-reaching goals.

Much as we would like to be able to make detailed plans and then cause them to come to fruition, it is much more likely that we will be given many more opportunities to react than to engineer or create.

Working to create flexibility, trying to keep options open, building networks, basic skills, balanced life elements are all career strategies that are realistic and productive. Setting up clever tactical career moves is not what makes career strategies work.

> **Instead of making the big splash with our lives, it could well be that the small substantial ripples will be our contributions.**

> **Change is a constant. A career strategy that is open to change is more likely to work long term than one with fixed, far-reaching goals.**

Many people have done the classic corporate tour de force only to discover, having lived in ten different cities and having paid the price in travel and endless hours, that the rewards in any form have eluded them.

The corporate piece of the mosaic can be a valuable one, but it is only a piece. It can't be the complete picture. The sooner you acknowledge the value of each element you are working with, the better. It is never too late to reassess what you are doing and make changes. Career strategies mean so much more than pursuing a career path. They more realistically involve the identification of what you can do at various stages of your life. The entire process is dynamic. Both you and your environment are in motion. Static strategies won't work. The ten steps to career success are fiction. The ten thousand situations they must address won't match up.

> **The corporate piece of the mosaic can be a valuable one, but it is only a piece. It can't be the complete picture.**

> **It is never too late to reassess what you are doing and make changes.**

> **Static strategies won't work. The ten steps to career success are fiction.**

> **Self-determination has always been an option in career strategies.**

YOUR LIFE'S MOSAIC

What works is a constant spirit of inquiry. What can I do today that will further my contribution? What can I learn? Who can I meet? How can I increase the quality of what I do? How can I increase the quality of my life? How can I increase the quality of life for others?

Each of the mosaic pieces must be crafted before they can be put together. Building quality parts will have a great deal to say about the overall picture that will result.

Sometimes we see the picture in great detail and sometimes we see only portions with no idea of how it will all come out. A few pieces added or subtracted here or there change everything.

Career strategies, of course, require concrete, not artistic, decisions. Do I leave or stay? Do I go in this direction or that? Am I in the right place? Should I follow this person or that? Whose advice should I take? Where can I get more data?

To build practical day-to-day skills in career strategies, you must practice the discipline in small ways all the time. You must take the time to read, to search, to work with others, to build contacts, to do all of the things that put you in control of the decision-making process. When you do the little things well, the big things get easier. Fortunately, you don't need a grand strategy. You don't need a wall chart of projected moves. You don't have to restructure your life in order to develop workable career strategies. You do have to stop and think about what you are doing. You do have to get others involved in your thought processes. You have to be receptive to change. You have to build breathing space into your career options. You have to look beyond the day-to-day, but not into the deep space of the future. Having some idea of where you are going short term will increase your likelihood of getting there.

Those who set strictly material goals often leave behind vast arrays of possessions. There is much more to life than acquisition. Your career strategies need to have broader objectives. They have to take in all of the factors of your life.

> **When you do the little things well, the big things get easier.**

> **Experiencing life as a spectator sport is a far riskier strategy than getting your hands on the controls and seeing where you can take yourself.**

Material well-being, physical and mental health, responsibilities for others, the different stages of life, the changing times are not checklist items. They are weighted segments that increase and decrease as we progress through our careers.

No one has all the answers, and you will not have them either. That's not what you are seeking. Your strategies should be directed at goals that are meaningful to you. They should be in time segments that are manageable. They will shift when least expected. They will achieve results in direct proportion to your input.

We are each unique individuals. We must make our way in a plural society. Our career strategies must reflect both factors. What do we have to offer? Where will what we do provide the desired return? Those two questions and the multiple and changing answers they produce are what will shape our future. If you want to have a greater influence on your future, just come up with better answers to those questions. You can ask them and answer them as many times as you would like.

Self-determination has always been an option in career strategies. Many have elected to leave that option in the hands of organizations or others. They have decided to see what happens. They have become spectators, watching their own careers. Whether it is fear of failure, satisfaction with early progress, or a lack of confidence, experiencing life as a spectator sport is a far riskier strategy than getting your hands on the controls and seeing where you can take yourself.

Freedom of choice is greater than it has ever been, and it seems to be increasing all the time. It is a two-edged sword that must be grasped and wielded with care. If not grasped, you can merely admire its potential. If taken in hand, its potential then can be transformed into reality.

Who would have ever speculated even a few short years ago that three, four, and five careers might be available to almost anyone?

Who would have been able to predict all of the variable life situations that would be opened as a result of technology, transportation, and communications progress?

Who would have guessed how the pieces of their career mosaic would have come together to form the picture of their present day lives?

Identifying and putting those pieces together is the challenge of this book. Writing the chapters of your autobiography is the challenge of your personal book about your career strategies after thirty-five.

> **Freedom of choice is greater than it has ever been.**

MORE GOOD BOOKS FROM WILLIAMSON PUBLISHING

AFTER COLLEGE
The Business of Getting Jobs
by Jack Falvey

Wise and wonderful . . . don't leave college without it. Filled with unorthodox suggestions (avoid campus recruiters at all costs!), hands-on tools (put your money in stationery, not in resumes), wise observations (grad school? - why pay to learn what others are paid to learn better). You've already spent a fortune on textbooks. Now for only $10 you can have the most valuable book of all.

192 pages, 6 x 9
Quality paperback, $9.95

INTERNATIONAL CAREERS:
An Insider's Guide
by David Win

If you long for a career that combines the excitement of foreign lifestyles and markets, the opportunity to explore your own potential, the promise of monetary and personal reward, then learn from David Win how to get off the stateside corporate ladder and into the newly emerging areas of international careers. Now's the time!

224 pages, 6 x 9, charts
Quality paperback, $10.95

CAREER DIRECTORY SERIES
Advertising   **Public Relations**
Book Publishing   **Newspaper Publishing**
Magazine Publishing   **Marketing**

Each directory contains many, many informative, eye-opening articles written specifically for these directories by the top CEO's in each field from the big name companies. Complete breakdown of job specialization in each career field. List of company policies, personnel procedures, key contacts, internships. Excellent. Does all the leg-work for you and tells how to get a foot in the door.

375–400 pages, 8½ x 11
Quality paperback, $17.95 each

HOW TO IMPORT A EUROPEAN CAR
The Gray Market Guide
by Jean Duguay

Here's everything you need to know to purchase a car in Europe, drive it on your vacation, and ship it legally into the United States. You can save up to 25% on foreign car purchases—at the very least pay for your whole trip in savings! Names, addresses for reliable European dealers, best U.S. conversion centers, shippers. Covers DOT, EPA, customs, financing, bonding. Cost comparison for 200 models. Authoritative.

192 pages, 8½ x 11, illustrated, tables
Quality paperback, $13.95

DINING ON DECK:
Fine Foods for Sailing & Boating
by Linda Vail

For Linda Vail a perfect day's sail includes fine food—quickly and easily prepared. She offers here 225 outstanding recipes (casual yet elegant food) with over 90 menus for everything from elegant weekends to hearty breakfasts and suppers for cool weather sailing. Her recipes are so good and so varied you'll use her cookbook year-round for sure!

160 pages, 8 x 10, illustrated
Quality paperback, $9.95

THE CAMPER'S COMPANION TO NORTHERN EUROPE
A Campground & Roadside Travel Guide

THE CAMPER'S COMPANION TO SOUTHERN EUROPE
A Campground & Roadside Travel Guide
by Dennis & Tina Jaffe

More than just campground directories, these travel guides share the best of each country off-the-beaten path. The Jaffes rate over 700 campgrounds covering all of Northern Europe in one volume, Southern and Eastern Europe and Northern Africa in the other volume. Country-by-country campgrounds.

300 pages, 6 x 9, maps, tables
Quality paperback, $13.95 each

GOLDE'S HOMEMADE COOKIES

by Golde Hoffman Soloway

"Cookies are her chosen realm and how sweet a world it is to visit."
Publishers Weekly

Over 100 treasured recipes that defy description. Suffice it to say that no one could walk away from Golde's cookies without asking for another . . . plus the recipe.

144 pages, 8¼ x 7¼, illustrations
Quality paperback, $7.95

SIMPLY ELEGANT COUNTRY FOODS:
Downhome Goes Uptown

by Carol Lowe-Clay

An outrageously good cook brings country cooking to its pinnacle. A cookbook that's not fussy, not trendy - simply elegant. Everything from country fresh Pizza Rustica to Crumbed Chicken in Wine Sauce, Country Pork Supper, Sweet Cream Scones with Honey Butter to Whipped Cream Cake with Almond Custard Filling. Over 100 recipes capturing the freshness of the moment!

160 pages, 8 x 10, beautifuly illustrated
Quality paperback, $8.95

ICE CREAM!
The Whole Scoop

by Gail Luttmann

Ice cream lovers rejoice! Here are over 250 unbelievably delicious, homemade ice cream recipes including frozen custard, tofutti, ices, sherbets, sorbet, low-fat, low-cholesterol ice cream, sauces, ice cream cakes, ice cream for diabetics, and more. For every kind of ice cream freezer!

220 pages, 8 x 10, photos
Quality paperback, $10.95

TO ORDER

At your bookstore or order directly from Williamson Publishing. We accept Visa or Mastercard (please include number, expiration date and signature), or send check to **Williamson Publishing Co., Church Hill Road, P.O. Box 185, Charlotte, Vermont 05445**. (Phone orders: 802-425-2102.) Please add $1.50 for postage and handling. Satisfaction guaranteed or full refund without questions or quibbles.